God's Got an App for That!

To Tara

Because of His Dead Love we have great grace.

Doris Bedsole

1

Published by:

Elk Mountain Books
info@perryperkinsbooks.com

Copyright © 2016 by Doris Bedsole
ISBN Print Edition: 1500965723
EAN-13: 978-1500965723

What Others Are Saying...

Inspiring! A message from the Lord written as a modern parable. God is in control!

Perry P. Perkins
CEO
MY KITCHEN Outreach Program

`````````````````````````````````````````````````````

Presents a good argument a personal relationship is possible with the Almighty!

Ron Stacy author of *"The Covenant Factor"*

`````````````````````````````````````````````````````

A testimony of the author's painful but rewarding pilgrimage towards a more mature, trusting relationship with our tripartite Lord, Father, Son and Holy Spirit.

Her poignant word pictures are pregnant with practical applications of Godly wisdom. Her stories of God's miraculous provision and healing intervention are faith building and inspiring. You will grow to trust Him more as you read.

Get ready for life change. You won't want to put this book down!

Larry Kennedy
Pastor
Author, *"I Tell You the Truth"*

Acknowledgements

I, as much as anyone know you cannot accomplish life alone.

I have to acknowledge God first because this book is all about Him interacting with my life for the better. I have to thank my husband Steve and 5 children James, Michelle, Bridgette, Brenda and Steve II, for putting up with me.

No one is sadder for my short falls or happier for the moments I actually did well for you. You are all awesome.

I have to thank my best friend Laurie Kennedy for her friendship and encouragement. I am very appreciative of Ray and Debi Birch for their belief in me as an author. Every time we met they would call me an author out loud and my heart would jump. I have to thank my Gathering Ladies for their constant support and prayers. You are such a huge part of my even understanding my story.

Thank you Paul Young, Baxter Kruger and John MacMurray for the encouragement, that our stories are important and valuable to Kingdom life.

Nadine Zook you are a wonderful book cover designer. First you are a great and generous friend.

Perry Perkins thank you for being a good friend and all the work you did to bring this book together. Thank you for not losing patience with me.

TABLE OF CONTENTS

5

GOD'S INSPIRATION FOR THIS BOOK

Lately, whenever I talk about what I am looking for, my kids seem to say, "There's an app for that." It is a lot of fun to get quick answers to life's searches, and having the ability to search for what I need in my pocket on this little device anytime day or night is very empowering.

If you have checked your smartphone lately you know it is so true. Need a light? There's an app for that. What is the price of something and where can I find it? There's an app for that.

Where am I, where is a good restaurant, coupons, weather? Yep, there's an app for that.

We are in an era where our upgraded communication systems are significantly important to conducting our lives in an effective manner. Not to mention how safe I feel knowing I can call for help and get it quickly.

During a recent time of worship, I was preoccupied with contemplating some issues in my life. God broke in with, "I have an app for that." Needless to say, I shook my head in disbelief at what I had just heard go through my mind. My response was the dubious, "WHAT?"

"I have an app for that."

Then a flood of questions went through my mind, and to all of them, He answered, "I have an app for that."

Got sin and guilt?

"I have an app for that. A savior. Redemption."

Need beauty for ashes?

"I have an app for that. Born-again."

Need healing and wholeness?

"I have an app for that. 'By His stripes and the word of my testimony, and the blood of the lamb.'"

Feel lost and alone?

"I have an app for that. I will never leave you. My spirit is in you."

Need wisdom?

"I have an app for that. I give wisdom generously to those who ask."

Need to know how to do something?

"I have an app for that. I have given you the anointed mind of Christ."

Then He said, "Some of my people are still only connected to landlines, not realizing their limitations. Some of them have little flip phones, which is an improvement, but not enough for what is to come. I need my people to get smartphone capacity, to upgrade their communication skills with me. I need to be able to more readily download to them what is needed when they need it."

The Lord may speak more to you than to me about this. My take on this is the landlines represent a need to have to take people somewhere, like church, or someone you think is more connected to God than you to be ministered to because you don't know who you really are and the power God has given you for such a time as this. Perhaps reciting a prayer, you learned instead of open communication with God.

Flip phones are people who don't mind administering a simple prayer they learned somewhere, which is good start maybe, but the need for a touch and a word from God requires so much more.

Being the upgraded communication version of a smartphone is you being what you and other people need when it is needed, with power. You become the hotline to God, the red phone between heaven and earth.

The titles of the chapters in this book are the apps God brought to me. I have been asked by many people to write the story of my life. I have not wanted to do that because in my thinking, I don't know who would be interested in buying a book about me. One day, I told my friend Debbie about the word I received from Papa. As I was telling her, His words went through my head, "That's the book you're going to write. The book is not about you, it is about Me and who I am in your life and what I have done. This is our story, not just yours."

All I could do then was bid good-bye and humbly walk away. I recognized He was large and in charge, and I am not. As much as I would like to think I made the right choice choosing Him, the reality is He tracked me down in hot pursuit of the one He decided to love. In these chapters are my experiences with a living God, and His living word having its way in me, ready or not—usually not.

There are many stories here that are my stones of remembrance. In the Old Testament days, they would build a pile of rocks they called altars over every encounter with God. These stones served as a reminder of the power of God in their lives every time they passed by. When their children and grandchildren passed by, they would ask, "What is this one for?" The stories would be told again and again of the greatness of God in their lives. This remembrance would stir love and faith in God in them. It would also give them courage to face the next challenge because here was proof God was there for them when they turned to Him. If you are new to the family of heaven, you may not have many stories of your encounters with God yet.

The stories of others who have gone before you can raise up faith in you to trust God for your answers. It is kind of like having Wi-Fi on your phone and others can pick up on your connection. That only happens on smartphones.

When I was born-again, I began to carry the kingdom and the presence of God and the power of the King in me wherever I went. I did not understand that during most of my Christian walk. Now I see that I was an unschooled child in the ways and rights of the family I was just adopted into. This was OK since I was not mature enough to handle it properly. Once I had grown in the Lord some and received the truth, I became in a sense a Wi-Fi hotspot, in keeping with this smartphone theme. My communication lines are more open, clear, and able to download what God has for me or for another person in that moment. I can either remember my faith story or someone else's, or a prophetic word will come to encourage my life or someone else's life. I have found we all need confirmation that God is listening and is our ever present help in time of need. You and I need to believe that with all that is within us. Our corner of the world needs us to. Remember we are to be broken bread and poured out wine to those around us, like Jesus. I am sharing my story here in this book and wherever I go. God is making a story in you, too. Share it. A metaphor you may be able to understand is we are the wet nurses of the new babies in faith. If those you encounter are not yet born-again, then you are the midwife for a child of God to enter the kingdom. God is in charge of the miracle of life. We can't save anyone. Jesus did it already.

An important part of that word was God needs us to upgrade our communication skills. There is no condemnation for where you are currently in your communication skill. It is just time to know you need to pursue the upgrade. I found every stage of communication is just that, a stage you go through and then you grow to the next stage. Babies cry and make noises to communicate. They progress to one and two syllable words to get a need met. Grade school children can say much more, but their concerns are still mostly self oriented. I had to decide to reach for growing up and developing an understanding of the stuff of life. I grapple with finding out the truth about God and what relationship with Him can mean. Maturity in age as well as spiritually brings you to a place where you can handle responsibility for yourself and then begin to help others. I needed to choose to be willing to take on the responsibility of representing the real God. The one whose love for us is exceedingly extravagant in His own way. He does have His own way of doing things.

It is imperative for my survival and yours that we find intimate relationship with our Lord, who holds every answer for our life. We have all learned to self-protect our core intimate places, some more than others—for good reasons, I know. I had to press in to know Him before my heart and soul would surrender to such a relationship with Him, or anyone. Wherever we were wounded growing up is where we get stuck. We pick up many not so true perceptions about life that hinder us from seeing the true God. It was a tremendous paradigm shift in relationship to God for me, one I began by tiptoeing in. I thought He made the world then abandoned us to our own devices.

Jesus paid the full price for you and me to have the best of communication upgrades for our well-being. We need only accept Him and begin to accept His truth about us and the world around us to enter into the most peaceful and powerful life. Joyce Meyer once said, "Worry was worship of another God." Oswald Chambers called fretting, "Making plans without God." "So True," says me. God says I have a plan for your future, for your welfare, NOT your destruction. Sometimes you wonder at the look of things. This is where faith and trust come in. What father would give his child a rock if he asked for bread? Trust was the original problem we had in the

11

Garden of Eden. The serpent cast doubt that God was good and had the best intentions for them. He urged them to become their own god by eating the fruit of the tree of good and evil. News flash: we won't ever know better than Papa God.

Our heavenly Father, God, is ever increasing his manifold glory to us, in us, and through us, to the family and to all the people on the planet. My definition of manifold resembles a fan that keeps unfolding, keeps revealing more and more.

I have this awareness we are on the clock, so to speak, the heavenly clock. Our time in pursuit of relationship with Him is crucial. He is with us in laughter and in tears, in every circumstance of life. I so encourage you to engage Him! Don't just let Him be a spectator, and then you wonder what went wrong and why He didn't do something you wanted Him to. He is not the magic blessing genie at your command. He is the best Dad and the author and finisher of our faith. We learn some of our best lessons about the truth of God and who He is in a relationship when things go sideways and upside down. In this world, you will have tribulation, He said. At one point when all seemed lost, someone told me education is very expensive. Not all education happens in a school building. Teachers come in many forms. Try spitting into the wind and see what you learn.

I have a little sign posted on the slanted ceiling of my attic office/craft room. Written by Philip Brooks, it says:

>Never pray for an easier life,

>Pray to be a stronger person.

>Never pray for a task equal to your power,

Pray for power equal to your task.

Then your work will be no miracle,

YOU will be the miracle!

When things get messy, I gotta ask myself, did I go to my Jesus app (talk to God) and find out what He has in mind for whatever issue is on my plate? I have to monitor myself. Did I go there and employ His method? Or did I think He was supposed to make my way work? He is creating a people who have right priorities and pursue higher calls. He has a bigger agenda to account for!

I may or may not hear the answer, but it will be evident I got one eventually, like it or not. Sometimes the lesson was just to get me to let go and trust. If I get mad or depressed about an answer, it was because I wanted to hang onto something that was ultimately not going to serve my life with Him. It would probably only have gotten in the way of the next best thing.

I am not writing this because I am laying claim to being an expert. I can no more explain God than Job could in the middle of his trouble. In Chapter 38 of Job, God calls him out for trying. So where were you, dude, when the heavens were measured or stars installed in the sky? Did I consult you on how high to make mountains? I don't want to find myself on that carpet in any position.

I am trying to report what I have found to be true. God asked me to write this book, so I am being obedient. I am counting on His council for the whole thing. We all need to examine everything we read or hear and ask God to confirm it before we take it in as part of our belief system.

I have put in scriptures for reference, because I believe I have to run my experiences through the Word and make sure I don't jump to conclusions and misinterpret God's working in my life. Hopefully, I am interpreting accurately. You need to take it all to your prayer time, your conversation with God.

I have found Him to be an in-dwelling, life giving, answer-oriented, and adventurous Father God. His answers for your every moment will bring peace and every fruit of the spirit. The fruit of the spirit seems to be the outcome of asking for His Spirit to be born in you. His Spirit reproduces His attributes in you (just for the record, they are love, joy, peace, kindness, faithfulness, longsuffering, gentleness, and self-control). He will bring things that far exceed your imagination, way more what you really want than what you *think* you want. You haven't seen all the choices yet or what is on the agenda. These attributes bring heaven to earth. Let Your kingdom come, Lord, Your will be done on earth as it is in heaven.

What is happening in your moment today? What do you need from your loving and nurturing Daddy God? He has an app for that. Call Him and upgrade to the heavenly smartphone he has waiting just for you, and get your download of what you need every moment, today and every day.

Dee Bedsole (& the Holy Spirit) July 4th, 2012

14

SIN AND GUILT

I know my fair share about how the sin and guilt cycle can eat at you. I used to think sin was something I did. Walking down this path with God, it turns out to be a different story.

Our great grandparents inadvertently chose that for us. By grandparents I mean Adam and Eve. It is our inheritance from them. Sin turned out to be the nature I was born with and practiced as naturally as breathing.

They introduced sin nature into the world when they decided to believe the serpent instead of God. At that moment, they chose a different master. Adam and Eve, like every other parent, passed down family traits. Sin is part of the only perspective someone born into this world knows. It is like being born and raised in a mud puddle.

Mud is all you know until you see or experience something different. Spiritually speaking, it is your born-again experience. Once that happens, you have to choose which life you want to live. As I read the Bible, it seemed to me that most human beings practiced a mindset of, "I can go my own way and do my own thing with little regard to God or other people."

It certainly was true of me. Oswald Chambers says sin is self-realization that leads to "I am my own god. To me be the glory for the things I have done."

In case you haven't noticed, if you have a child, you need to train them to care and think about others. Remember, all their toys are MINE, MINE, MINE. All of humanity's best efforts seem to only produce the collective idea of good human standards, and we are not all that good as a people. If you have checked history, the moral compass shifts back and forth like a pendulum when left to the collective. When left to the collective, a civilization usually progresses to a certain point then gets bloated on itself and starts going downhill. That is how history appears to me. History books tell you history tends to repeat itself.

Growing up, I never felt like I belonged anywhere. I was always on the outside looking in. I was a visitor passing through, with no attachments to people or things. My parents were too busy, too tired, or too mad at something to connect relationally. Now that I am grown up, I would say they were preoccupied with their own issues. I certainly have been guilty of that with my own children. I was told by my parents that their issues *and* my issues were my fault. It seemed there was no one in my corner, no one for me. I wasn't even sure *I* was for me.

Mom never even clued me in on the facts of life. Thank God for high school biology. The only conversations I remember with my Dad happened while we did dishes together. Usually it was, "Don't make your mother mad," or "Hurry up." Then there were the off-color stories and jokes, so very inappropriate to tell a young girl. I was very confused by those at the time.

By the time I reached my twenties, my responses to life were pretty wild. I had already been told I was bad, for what I wasn't sure, and I judged myself bad for all my actions. Looking back at my life, I can see I lived out of that place of believing I was bad, sinful, and no good thing could come from me. In counseling, I have learned so much about my childhood wounds. All the separateness and lack of connecting has been from a lack of bonding to anyone early on. So many feelings of being bad and a mountain of fears come from this "lack of the necessary good" place. Even as an adult, my self-protection mechanism kept me from close relationships, even from the closeness I wanted so much with my husband and children. This fear robs you of so much of the richness of your life.

I didn't care much about me as a young adult, so why should anyone else. I was carrying so much guilt and shame. I learned free love in the 1960s was never free. It came with a high diminishing return on my self-concept and self-respect! SELF-RESPECT—what in the world was that?! My life was more about having guilt to bear and shame to hide. I had no instruction from my parents on life. I guess they thought I would figure it out on my own or they would keep control. It was like being dropped in the forest with no survival training, no supplies, and no compass.

The human survival instinct is a really fascinating mechanism.

I tried selling myself a story of who I thought I could be. This was someone I really wasn't. Total hogwash. It is what sin does, it covers itself. Adam and Eve tried leaves.

To your own self be true may not be scripture, but it is a wise saying to think about. The worst lie you tell is the one you tell yourself and then swallow hook, line, and sinker. I decided I was a liberated, cool, and savvy woman. I was a club dancer, selling drugs, and myself upon occasion, as the need arose.

The ugly details will probably get told if anyone ever asks me, or maybe in another book. For now, it is a collection of stories that would take us away from the point of this chapter and this book, which I think is God is not who I thought He was and neither am I. Neither is sin.

The proverbial pendulum would eventually swing back, and horrible guilt and shame would consume me from time to time. I sometimes would think of the good people I knew and wonder what they thought of me. Then I would make myself feel better by saying I was living free. No social rules limiting my actions. I could do whatever I felt like. The trouble with that was I only felt like doing things that made more problems for me and everyone else. That was my selfish inherited sin nature, alive and kicking.

It is interesting to look back and see how driven I was by my belief system. I am still driven by a belief system, it's just a different one now. When I believed I was bad, I made bad choices. When I wanted to convince myself I was good enough, I would do some good deed. It made me believe and feel I had satisfied some inner requirement, proving I had some good in me. However, a few good deeds here and there did not make me a good person. There was and still is none noticeably good but God. Oswald Chambers says, "The true test of the Christian character is not good-doing but God likeness.

God life in us expresses itself as God life, not as humans trying to be godly." It seems important to figure out the difference in order to be in right relationship.

I need to say here, I have found trying to be good person was not what God is looking for anyway. Are you surprised by that? I was. God was looking for a relationship with me right where I was. His desire was for me, and for me to respond to His love for me. Responding to His love would let love mold me if I was willing to be wet clay in His hands, as in Isaiah 64:8. From this place of love and acceptance in our relationship, His hope is we will recognize the privilege and joy of this blessing and pass it on.

Just like my natural family habits can be changed through conscious efforts and hard work, my sin nature can be altered by other kinds of conscious acknowledgements, such as accepting the all-inclusive and finished work Jesus did on the way to the cross and His resurrection. Add to that the acceptance of my place in the family of God. Of course, then there is God's way of doing things. I had to be willing to participate in the relationship to be transformed by it. To paraphrase John 1:12, to those who believe, God gives the **power to become** children of the living God. It is only God in you that can do this. It isn't just saying the magic words; there is a real process. If you won't admit the fact you are sick, you won't receive the help you really need to be well. Papa wants you to have wholeness and wellness.

Do you love anyone who is not always good? That would be everyone in my life. How about you? God's love is unconditional, and that is the source of my love. I love that God declares Himself true love, because that love makes me Holy. No human act can make you Holy. God decided He would love you and die for you before the foundations of the earth, before you were born. Holy is set aside for God. You decide if you will let yourself be set aside for God. It is an invitation into what has already been done. Your choice is to enter into relationship and blessing or stay out in the rain. What made the Holy Family Holy? Jesus was in it!

Not everyone I love knows Jesus. I aim at reflecting that love to them no matter what they do or say. I am not always good at it. Hopefully, one day, it will encourage them to want relationship with a God who is kind to the broken and lame. I hope I am being transformed into the taste of God in their life. "Oh, taste and see that the LORD *is* good." (Psalm 34:8) I have realized that if those of us who have tasted and seen don't serve up a taste, the people around us don't get it.

It is kind of like when you watch a movie about a love story.

I remember watching *The Notebook*. It is the only movie that ever brought tears to my husband's eyes. We both knew each of us wanted a love like that. A love so devoted that even when things were less than ideal, or were going downhill, it's there for you.

The one who loves you and me sacrificed his life to prove it. He will always be there for us. He always has my best interest at heart, an important truth to remember even when it doesn't look like it. Jesus waits patiently for me to finally grasp the value of His truth.

Declaring the truth to myself in the face of the lies the enemy of my soul and the world around us tell is the only defense that overcomes.

I am not completely transformed yet. When I allow it, God will always work a good deed through my life. I still find I have to wrestle parts of me down to accept anonymity. The little girl inside me so wants that instant recognition from others. She wants a gratuitous response more than equal to the deed. A deed, may I remind you, that was inspired by the Spirit of God, empowered by God, and sponsored by God. I was fortunate enough to be there. When I get past that desire for recognition, I will have some more maturity, at least in that area. I wish maturity and transformation happened all at once, but they seem to come one at a time, and then again, in layers. I read in the Bible that we are built line upon line, precept upon precept. That has been true so far. I wish it were page by page or book by book. Line by line seems so slow. I guess I should be grateful it didn't say word by word.

I used to blame all the bad on God instead of the devil and his minions, and my susceptible woundedness would feed on the lies the enemy told me. He lies on both ends of the spectrum. He is either telling you how you're bigger than life, so slick, deserve so much more and it doesn't matter how you get it, or he says, "You're bad," "You're a failure," "You're not smart enough to do that," "Be afraid to risk," "Don't talk to people, they will betray you," and "Trust no one."

The lack of bonding and not getting the necessary good early on in life brings all those thoughts to mind. The enemy of your soul is right there to confirm and prove it to you. Your best weapon is the truth about the nature and character of the God who loves you! Call on Him and ask. There is an app for that. The sheep know His voice, and He is ready to answer when you call.

I have learned to trust people to be human and for God to be God. I am learning to evaluate people by their level of spiritual maturity in correlation to their humanity. I am thinking that's about values and self-control. I have learned no matter what people do to hinder or hurt me, my Papa is there as my ever present help. He turns what was meant to be evil toward me into something good.

Our orderly Father set up in the universe a means of learning by consequence that teaches us through experience what works and what doesn't. Some of us have been burned by fire and know not to do that again, or at least to be far more careful.

I have found that casting your bread on the water and having it come back tenfold is a force to be reckoned with. I have paid dearly for bad choices made out of my own limited knowledge and reasoning.

The grief that starting sexual activity in high school brought on my life was huge. I was nowhere near ready to handle the emotions or responsibility that come with it. There is nothing casual about sex. I have met so many Christians who don't get the importance of restraint in this area of their life. On the other end of the spectrum, I have also met many women who have a very tainted idea of even participating in sex with their husbands. It is so sad to see what the enemy of the soul has done to this beautiful, exotic gift God has given us. Perhaps one day God will let me write a little book about that.

I used to hang out with people who partied hard and cast off all restraint. It seriously altered my view of what is appropriate behavior. Not that I ever really had any idea of such a thing! I know there are many definitions out there about what appropriate behavior is. Even among churches there are huge differences. I now concern myself with what God thinks when He looks at me, not man, nor church rules. I lean a lot on scripture that talks about whatever you do, do it unto God. It covers a multitude of issues for me, like tattoos, food, dress, words of your mouth, and activities. It seems everything with God is about why you do or don't do it.

Back in my party hardy days, modesty was not a concern in the way I dressed, and the way I talked began to be filled with colorful swear words.

Someone reading this might not know Jesus yet and are wondering what is wrong with that. First thing I would like to say is God is not freaked out by swear words, or anything else you do or say. He told me that blessing is better than cursing any day. The question is what do I want in my life, to be blessed or cursed? He has seen it all many times over. I have learned from Him that my life is better spent involved in what I am for than what I am against. He knows that speaking blessings and positive affirmations are better for me in my life and better for the people in and around my life.

Ray Hughes once said that if we only knew the power in our blessing we would say a blessing with our every step. The Bible says the earth is groaning waiting for us to take our rightful place of authority on the earth.

His main concern is that we get into a personal interactive relationship with Him, and then as a branch of His tree, we are able to be fruitful and multiply and spread His blessing on the earth.

My words do create my atmosphere. I have noted how if I believe my first grumpy critical thought in the morning, I can make a miserable day for myself. If I stop and take a minute to invite God in, get my attitude of gratitude going, and thank Him for some things, it all turns out much better.

I heard about an experiment that was done with two bowls of rice. Students would say good things to one bowl and they would yell at and say mean things to the other. The bowl that got the cursing turned black and the other stayed white. I can't verify this story, but I do compliment the plants in my kitchen. Yes, I talk to them. I bless them with twinkle lights and nice music, too. Some think my kitchen looks like an oversized terrarium. In the winter, I can still get the garden feeling in my kitchen. It is a happy place for me. Not everyone's forte.

You may have noticed how people who participate in activities like I did in my wild era are not the most reliable, truthful, or trustworthy. A loyal relationship without a personal agenda is not in their makeup. Their priorities are usually selfish in nature. If you think they did something just for you, look a little deeper. There is usually a string attached so they can manipulate you in the future, or they did it to make themselves feel good about themselves—"Look what I did." When push comes to shove, they will be back to get recompense for the good deed. You will hear, "Remember when I did one good thing? You owe me." After a while, you believe everyone is like that. That is one of those lies the enemy of the soul affirms to keep you isolated and in self-protect mode. The problem is it carries over into your relationship with God. He is the one person you desperately need to learn to trust. His agenda is to deeply love you and draw you into the sweetest relationship you will ever know.

When tragedy happens, the biggest question everyone asks is why didn't God stop this bad thing from happening in my life, since he is all knowing and all powerful? You and I have no idea how painful it is for Him to let us live with our **free will** and suffer the consequences that go with our choices.

Did you get that? He let you have free will and face your consequences. Like every other parent, He would like to keep you from some of the pain of life. **His love for you holds Him in restraint** because love does what is really needed. What teaches better than a consequence? I don't like that His love has mercy and respects the free will of perpetrators as well as victims. I am sure my kids have the same question for God as I did: "God, why didn't you give me better parents?" He created a natural order, parents were supposed to get with God and pass on His love, acceptance, wisdom, kindness. Sorry, it all went sideways. Just as in the beginning Adam and Eve believed the lie the serpent told them, casting doubt on the goodness of God, so did our other ancestors. Instead of worshiping love and truth, we decided as human civilization to go for comfort and selfish ambitions.

How difficult it is for Him to step in when we insist on believing the lies instead of the truth about who He is, who we are, and the power we have over our own lives. I have found Him merciful. Many a consequence could have been much worse without His mercy. **His desire for me and you is that we recognize our power**, not for Him to take it away from us. He is always placing circumstances around you to cause you to reach for that power and use it. The enemy of your soul is the one who is trying to render us powerless victims of the circumstances of our life. Here is another good non-scripture one liner, "The best revenge is a better life."

I am not a religious theologian. I even need help to spell it. I am an average person just writing about what I have discovered in my pursuit of relationship with God. Following religious rules never gave me the sense of fulfillment that following God does.

I have experienced firsthand the amazing truth that love transforms people. It is a wonderful journey to be on, and it never ends for all eternity. I never realized that in my childhood, I had closed the front door of my heart, until the day I opened and let Jesus in. Now my journey finds me opening the closed doors of the rooms in my heart. Funny thing is, I never knew they were closed.

I love the study of quantum physics. It is the best explanation I have found to help me grasp how God is omnipotent yet chooses to mostly work through us and around us, never without us, even when we don't know him yet. He is my cause and effect these days. He has always been engineering circumstance to nudge me in a direction that would eventually bring me into a deeper and closer love relationship with him. I am always being wooed. One day it kind of hits you in the head, like "I could've had a V8," when you finally figure out what is going on.

I have power over any circumstance because I am a part of Him. "I am in Him and He is in me," as in John 14:20. I need to always keep finding out what it takes to get in tune with Him and learn to use it well. That would be another one of those maturity things.

He is always attempting to get me to a place of understanding the things of life. I am thankful for it, since my parents missed that part. I am betting that is why he made sure Proverbs got in the Bible.

When children are little, we hound them about brushing their teeth in hopes they will have good teeth. When they reach a certain age, they can choose not to brush for whatever reason and face the consequences. My firsthand experience is painful and expensive. Who loves a root canal or an extraction? If your children faked it when you were not looking, they are more likely to be slack about brushing when they grow up, because they are not mature in the care of their teeth and will therefore get cavities faster. My job as a parent was to communicate what is going on with brushing their teeth and hopefully get them to buy into the responsible idea of care for themselves and their teeth. It would make a huge difference if they can grasp the gravity of the situation, because if they do, it becomes their personal choice and they become self controlled and responsible about their own teeth. They now have power over the condition of their teeth. Since I am the mother of five and grandmother of eight, I have some experience to back this up.

If you only try to be good in order to prove you are good, and not living and doing out of your relationship with God, you will not be so good in the hidden places. I have learned everything hidden will sooner or later come to light.

Real tooth brushers have nice teeth; the fake tooth brushers don't usually. When my kids saw an uncle with really ugly teeth because he didn't care for them, they found all the cause they needed. Punishments rather than encouragements would have never accomplished this effect. I found help from Proverbs in the idea it is better to learn from others' mistakes than the pain of your own.

However, some of us just don't get it unless it's firsthand pain, like a root canal. Hope I didn't lose you in that example.

People forget God has a bigger picture to account for. Most children don't like facing up to their responsibility, let alone pay the consequences for it. That would include some of us big kids.

Parents can make a huge mistake when they don't let their children face the consequences of little mistakes, where they have small consequences. As we grow up, the "oops" in life get bigger, and so do the consequences. The other side of the coin is when the consequences the parents dish out are too big for the mistake. The child will reject the wisdom of the consequence and rebel, not learning anything. But they will take up an offensive stance that could hurt them the rest of their life. What you want is for them to learn something, not frustrate them. OK, I will now step off my soap box.

Our Papa God is the best Dad ever. When I look across my life, I can see that in spite of all the heartache and pain I have endured, God always brought me the easiest way I would come. I am the one who made it difficult, with my temperament. It is His kindness that leads all of us to reconsider our ways (repentance) and turn from them. I have definitely experienced this firsthand.

My thoughts and stones of remembrance may not be your perfect answer, but it is as much as I understand at this point. We each have to go to Papa for ourselves. When we get to heaven, offering excuses like saying "I heard it somewhere" won't cut it.

I have a lot of questions too. Why did I have messed-up parents? Why would they think they should trade me to the mafia when I was a seventeen-year-old virgin in exchange for lifetime security?

Why couldn't my parents teach me to think and problem solve instead of controlling me? It would have been nice to not have made so many mistakes before I finally figured stuff out. Why have I been in so many traffic accidents which were ot my fault?

Your issues may have been far worse than mine. My point here is we can't and won't understand everything. You and I are not God. There is so much that can only be grasped from His viewpoint. He is far above us, and His quantum spirit is in the minutest detail. Only God can do that. I must trust in Him as a good Father. He loved me all the way to the cross and back again (it is way farther than to the moon and back). I can rest in the fact that I can trust Him with my life. Yes, even in the midst of circumstances I don't like.

When I look back, it becomes obvious how my guardian angels kept me from many worse situations. Papa kept directing and moving me lovingly through parts of my self-inflicted disasters even long before I signed up for this relationship.

One time BC (Before Christ in my life), I bought a large quantity of drugs while I was attending a continuing education class at UC Berkley. I invited some teachers who were curious about drugs and wanted a controlled environment to try them out back to my hotel room. They were hungry, so I went for some snacks at the downstairs machine. On my way back, serious looking men in black suits got in the elevator ahead of me. Even though I was on LSD, I got in the elevator with an armload of snacks (dumb comes in many forms). The men in suits got out on my floor and trailed behind me down the hall. This made me get a little concerned. I then let the small group of men pass me, and they stopped in front of my door. I am sure you can imagine it was a very heart-stopping moment. However, they turned and went to the room across from mine. When the door opened, a grand cloud of smoke came billowing out and filled the hall. What a relief. They couldn't tell there was an equal amount of marijuana smoke leaking out of my room. While they were busy arresting my neighbors, I slipped into my room. I am not sure why, but I decided that must have been an act of the kindness of God. I had a soul-searching moment, earnestly considering to not be so brazen and maybe give up dealing drugs. If I had been arrested that day, it would have drastically changed my life and my testimony. I can only conclude it didn't fit in God's plan for my life.

How did that relationship with God happen?

I did finally figure out that the stuff I had been handed in my life was like trying to make a silk purse out of a sow's ear. Or make your Wal-Mart bag look like a Gucci. You get my drift. I tried many times for self-improvement. I finally realized that my occasional good deeds could not convince me I was a good enough person anymore. Then there was the determination to change my evil ways. I could never get it to work out for me. I could not shake the emotional pain I kept stuffing as I tried to ignore it. Can a person walk through a fire and ignore they are getting burned?

The despair in my emotional pain would uncontrollably pop out of me like a jack-in-the-box. I didn't know what to expect of myself. I often felt the hopelessness of a hamster on a wheel that doesn't go anywhere while life keeps throwing things at you. I couldn't seem to change anything about myself or my life for the better. It seemed everything I did to try to improve my life would lead me back to my pit. I knew there must be some trick to this good life thing that I was missing.

Providentially, I moved next door to a Good Samaritan family who also happened to be my landlords. So many things broke down in a short time. Manuel (his real name, and the Hispanic version of Emanuel—*God with us*) would come to fix everything with a huge smile. For some reason, I was annoyed anyone could be that happy all the time.

During all the repair work, they invited me to dinner and befriended me. I remember wondering why would they would invite someone like *me* to their table.

I observed real family for the first time. Manuel and his wife, Linda, loved and supported their children. There was intimate conversation between the children and them, filled with understanding, compassion, and instruction. I saw no yelling, no abuse. There I was at twenty-seven years old, jealous of what they had and with no idea how to get it.

One day, Manuel returned to check on my recently repaired stove. He walked in my door smiling as usual. I started to cry. He asked why I was crying, and I told him I didn't know. He said he knew "Today is the day Jesus is finally going to have you for Himself." I didn't really know what that meant, but as bad as I was feeling, I could roll with it.

I agreed to attend church that night with them.

Most of what the pastor said went right by me. I had no clue what he was talking about until I heard the preacher say **I could be born-again**. The words "new stuff" popped into my head. I could make a new life with new stuff. I could be a real Gucci bag! LOL.

I tried hard to white knuckle it and not get out of my seat and make a spectacle of myself going forward in a church. **I did not want a religion.** I only knew I was compelled to do this. I was still very hesitant to risk my heart to this God. I could not believe it when I popped out of my seat. At one point, I remember thinking, *Did someone stick a pin in my behind?* My feet seemed to be dragging me across the floor. The rest of my body was attached to my head, saying *NO, NO, NO don't go. Stay in your seat*.

When I got to the front of the church, the pastor asked me if I wanted to be born-again, start a new life, and ask Jesus into my heart for it to begin. I heard myself saying yes while my head said NO. Then the no stopped and something else began.

I had no clue what began or what it meant to ask Jesus into my heart. But I did know my heart needed help, and I knew I wanted a new lease on life.

In that instant, what I knew was **love** for the first time in my life. And I knew I would **never again be alone**. I dropped to my knees and cried. My heart and soul began to be so full and light! There ain't no love like the love of God. There seemed to be never ending buckets of tears and snot. All I could do was soak in His presence. When His heavy presence lifted, I could hardly walk out of the place. No more big empty hole inside me! Even in my best moments before that, something had always seemed to be missing. Not anymore!

I didn't get religion, I got a relationship, a Papa, a lover, a helper, and a protector. WOW!

If you're a Christian or not, most of you have at least heard that Jesus died for your sin. **Guilt and shame** were nailed to the cross along with Him. You've heard you were born-again. I heard all that too. What does that really mean? It can take you a lifetime to really get it. I didn't understand any more about that than I did about any relationship or marriage. It is a good thing His love relationship is a two-way street and God is willing to take the lead. He does know what makes a love relationship work. That is the process you go through, learning to accept His love and to love others His way.

It has taken a long time for me to get the truth of Him into the core of my being, where the true believer dwells. So often, I didn't feel His love. At times, I even felt like a phony. Sometimes, I had thoughts that I was acting out some fantasy and it wasn't real. I would have thoughts like, "What are you doing? This isn't real." There were so many thoughts that seemed to attack me. I learned to fight back, speaking the truth I had read about in the Bible. The support of Christian friends who would tell me about how they got through their experiences was so important.

It was a real battle for my mind, heart, and soul. The enemy of my soul will always be coming to steal the truth about who I am and what God has done for me. It is truth, not feelings, that need to rule my life. Believing the truth of God over the lies of the enemy is my number one job. It is imperative to believe with your every fiber that Jesus did a finished work. When Jesus said, "It is finished," that is exactly what He meant. You are no longer under the law of sin and death. You now have a clean slate. You live as a family member under love and grace. Apparently, the enemy's job is to steal the truth, steal my identity, and blind me to who God really is and who I am. Now I know to whom I belong.

I have come to be sorry for the person who thinks all the wonderful stuff they are holding onto could possibly be better than what Papa God wants to hand them. I had to empty my hands first, letting go of everything, before He could fill them up again. I still have to stop and check myself sometimes. I have a tendency to pick stuff back up that Jesus paid for; He will always want His stuff back.

Let's go back to the big night of accepting Him. I went home and got a great night's sleep. When I took a shower the next day, God decided He had something to say to me. What a surprise! The God of heaven also talks to us even in the shower. He said, "Everything you believe you know about yourself and the way you perceive the world around you is a lie."

You want to talk about being blown away.

Me: "God, I don't know how to act; I won't even know how to talk. What am I going to do?"

God: "Stay close."

Me: "God, hello, anything else?"

Since then, I have learned He may only use a few words, but they are always powerful. Also, He speaks when He wants to, which is not as often or as much as I would like.

I really wish my encounters with Him made an instant transformation in me. Then I could skip all the stupid stuff I am going to say and do next while I am in the learning curve. A friend of mine named George once said it's like the first gulp of hot coffee that is far too hot for human consumption—nothing you do next will be good. If you swallow, you will burn your gut; if you instantly spit it out, you spray the mess on the world.

I know I am not the best communicator. I need word pictures for a frame of reference. I appreciate Jesus using parables to communicate the concepts of truth to people. I am hoping my stories help you understand.

I would love to say I was walking the straight and narrow from that point. But no! I had to place my grappling hook in the truths I received and go through the process of getting from there to here. I still do that, because God is still revealing deeper truths. It appears the lies of the enemy are very much embedded deep into the soul, and getting the lies out and replacing them with truth in many cases can take almost as much time as the lie took embedding itself there in the first place.

I went backward a few times because the enemy is relentless, and I am sometimes so gullible about his lies. Every time I did go backward, I knew it was not the best choice for me, and I was very uncomfortable. Finally, I was beginning to know better, but I didn't just want better anymore, I wanted best. I encourage people to keep going for the best. Good, better, best, never let it rest, always let God make your good better and your better best. It's more non-scripture, but very wise, advice given to me in a commercial. Yes, you can glean God anywhere, especially in creativity.

For a long time, I looked at church as a necessary evil. You won't find that in the Bible, either. You *will* find the apostle Paul always busily teaching and correcting the new church. They had issues, too. All people have issues. There are no perfect people and no perfect churches. That is because, in case you hadn't noticed, the church is made up of people like you and me, flawed.

When I got saved, the church at large was little help. They were not as interested in a person's relationship with God as they were with how you looked and behaved. They seemed to focus on cloning people to be like them instead of like God, and then calling it Christianity. They spoke Christianese and did Christian type deeds. Remember, doing good deeds makes you feel and believe you are good. LOL. What was confusing to me was that they could be so very unkind about it.

At first, I did some church hopping to find out what was up with this church gig. I have figured out it is like any other household. The particular church follows the nature of the head of the house.

It seemed really crazy to me that so many of the people in the church (in general) and leadership were doing things that didn't line up with what they were preaching. At that time, I watched people walk away from God because someone they thought should know better did things not approved of by the others, or the church rule book, or moral failures.

I remember thinking how silly they were. I wasn't there because of anybody but God. Now how are we, including me, supposed to know better or want to be better if other people keep acting like this and going away? We need each other to get better. I need you to be here so I can get better. I could see God has put a piece of Himself in each of us that we need to share. I am trying to be there for you so you can get better too.

It was apparent to me that God was a whole lot more loving, forgiving, and kind than many church people or churches. So many acted like they thought they had it all together and should not be with those who didn't. I knew I didn't have it together and that I need help. In my lost feeling and thinking, I thought just about anybody would be doing this Christian thing better than me. I really believed that at the time. I also thought, *God, you've got a real problem here on earth! This lie thing is out of control.*

No doubt, they thought it was the best way to be for the time. Now I can see they were more into club rule-keeping than loving Jesus. Rules do make many people feel more secure. At that time, I had just started reading the Bible. I hadn't kept a rule in a long time, so the whole thing was making me dizzy.

People were so busy with the mess in their church, they didn't pay too close attention to my mess. That's OK, because God never lost sight of me. It wasn't too long before I started to feel the guilt of living with my boyfriend. God is kind like that, one thing at a time. It seemed strange at the time to feel that way, because I thought I had improved to be able to live with one man and be faithful to him. I thought it amazing I even thought like that, because it wasn't in my old nature. This is a testimony to the fact that my new nature (the born-again of the spirit me) was gaining a voice. The Spirit of God had moved in and begun to be fruitful and multiply His attributes in my spirit. I am happy to say I married my boyfriend. I was finally free to make the commitment, because I knew the God in me could keep it. I knew I wanted always to be loyal to this new love He had given me. "God is Love" (1John 4:8)is not His attitude, it is who He is.

It should always be that way in the family of God, with Papa and the Holy Spirit bringing the conviction to change. Jesus paid the ultimate price to have a say in my life. Our brothers and sisters should be the helpers giving the good news. You and I already know the bad news.

Sin, to me, is being out of relationship to God and doing things that are contrary to our own best interest and what Papa wants for us, which is only the best. That would be why we use the term "out of His will." I get this, because I have seen the examples of those uncles and aunts with the bad teeth of that destructive lifestyle. I have made a personal choice for my lifestyle. I hope you caught the analogy.

I never understood my need to be loved. I needed to recognize the difference between my affinity for someone and real love. God is love, and real love comes from God. When it comes to people falling in love and getting married, you'd better know the difference. Relationships always hit difficulty at some point. Unless you are pursuing God's heart in a matter, it may seem more trouble than it is worth. We as a people are a difficult bunch.

The old nature is so familiar and loud and demanding of its way. It can get hard to hear the still, small voice of God leading you into wisdom and truth. He has made provision, created a **Jesus app,** to destroy and remove sin and guilt from us. Remember, scripture says all judgment was rendered at the cross for all, and for all time. Jesus said it is finished. I don't think you can get any more final than that.

Papa always leads us in the **relationship app,** an app of love, joy, wholeness, and healing.

I hope you make the journey.

BEAUTY FOR ASHES

What a term, "beauty for ashes." I read *Angela's Ashes* by Frank Malacort. It was even better to listen to it on audio book. I loved his accent and his wit about what I call misfortune and tragedy. When you can make jokes about yourself and your life, I think you have crossed over into a place of healing. My life was not at all like Frank's, it does have some very challenging and colorful moments. I do hope I will continually grow, heal, and somewhat render that life tickling sense of humor when I talk to people.

Beauty for our ashes is one of the promises God gives us, written down in the Bible. My hope in writing anything down is to let people know who I have discovered God to be. I am also so grateful for my second chance at life and what He has done in it—be it the good, the bad, or the ugly—and for all He will do in the future. My other hope is whoever reads this finds hope for their life. He really does create beauty from ashes.

It helped me so much in the beginning of my walk with God to find someone else's real life story I could read while learning to relate to Father God. The Bible is the truth about God, but I needed to know about other people who found it true and still relevant today. I wanted to know it was really working.

I needed to know if I was the only one whose life was being intercepted by this God. I needed someone to reassure me I could trust my heart and my soul to this God. I hope this book might address that quest for you.

The really good news is, no matter where you were born, where you have been, who your parents are, what disaster has befallen you, or what bad decisions you have made, God CAN take that and create something beautiful with it. I must add here, most things take some time. Some things take a *really* long time to turn around. You have to be willing to walk through what it will take to change it. Life is not for the wimpy.

It is way better to be in the process and have that relationship of love with Papa God than anything else going on. I see so many people who are hiding in their pit, determined to hunker down in their misery, and you'd better not mess with it…or else. How sad, because God wants to lead them into real joy, but they insist on their misery. Beth Moore wrote a great book about getting up out of that pit. She is one of those who now makes some very funny stories out of her past misery. I hope to hug her one day, as a fellow overcomer.

As an adult now, much counseling and many acts of God later, I can look back and see my parents somewhat better, for who they really were. They have both passed, but not without their dramas.

I do not lay blame on them for my life. Any blame in this life belongs to the sin nature in us all and the fact we, as a people, have so fallen under the spell of the enemy lies about God and who we are. Generation after generation is getting farther and farther it seems from the truth and reality of God. We have been so very lost as a people, trying to put God into a neat box so we can control our experiences and our outcomes. My box for God's BC (before Christ) consisted of the thought that He made the world, then left the building. I see now that more reflected my abandonment issues than God's behavior.

We see so much lack in ourselves. Yes, I include myself in the we, how about you? I tried to fill it with drink, activity, perfectionism, critical judgments control, sickness, drugs, crafts, religion, reading, and a lot of other things. I am sure you could add a few for yourself. Many of these you really can't fault unto themselves as an activity. But there is a perversion that happens to them when they are a substituted for your real need.

All I really needed was to pursue what it takes to have an interactive personal relationship with Father God, Jesus, and the Holy Spirit. I needed to receive their love for me. I generally have the attention span of a gnat and the microwave answer syndrome. Relationship with anyone, including God, takes so much more. It is well worth the effort. Proverbs talks of the rewards of the pursuit of understanding. The Bible says to dwell in understanding. I strongly urge you to develop a mindset that is constantly updating your understanding of all things, especially God. These are fast-moving times we live in, our understanding and mindsets can become irrelevant practically overnight. We need constant upgrades to our smartphones and our knowledge of what is going on. True? Let's be real here, religion has not been honest with us about God. Religion hasn't even been honest with itself.

Frustration is eminent when you come to an absolute place about something. It closes the door for the whole truth. It is like believing a candle is the ultimate light. That works—until a greater light is discovered, then a greater one, and a greater one, and so on. The Son outshines them all.

I need a grip on right and wrong according to God, but love and understanding seems to trump it all with God. Not to bypass the principle of consequences for our actions, of course. Consequences, or reaping what you sow, has been the most prolific teacher for me. We do so much disservice to people when we do not permit a healthy level of consequence to be experienced. Of course, now you must discover the healthy definition of a healthy level.

Getting healthy in any area of your life can give you a run for your money, so to speak. I have found reading my Bible for information about God, as much as hearing from him, profitable. Reading books and talking to people helps to bring a greater dimension to what I think I know. There always seem to be aspects of the truth I have overlooked that others can direct me to. I know you have to beware, because some people will try to smack you upside the head with a truth they decide you need to know. I recommend remaining calm, saying thank you, and walking away. When you are alone with God, begin to master the art of bone picking, which is separating the edible parts and throwing the bones away. The God who loves you usually sends His truth with a tender touch, if you are receptive, and it will be a good thing to you to have the true answer. I have found that when I resist the truth, it is more like a slap in the face than a tender touch. I really need to get on my knees then.

I think that was a rabbit trail. I shall try to set the background of ashes for the canvas on which God will paint Himself beautiful. I guess this is the part where I tell my sad story. I know everybody has one.

In the beginning was God, then a few thousand years of history, and then there is my history.

On my dad's side of the family was grandpa Gregory, who came over from Sicily. He had four children when his wife died. He sent to Rome for one of his siblings' children, my grandma Rose. The deal was $250 and boat fare. She had been promised to a young man, but he had died in the war. She was nine then, so at age thirteen, with no other offers on the table, she became her first cousin's new bride. I used to like to use that as an excuse for all my stinkin' thinkin'. My dad was child number twelve in the lineup of seventeen children. He told me they ate breakfast at the Salvation Army before school every day. He only got to go to school up to sixth grade.

My grandfather's vocation was selling vegetables on street corners from a large wooden pushcart he made. My dad was pulled out of school to also push a cart and help support the family. As one child got old enough to get their own life, the next oldest child needed to step up and add to the family income.

I would like to see you try to sell that stream of thought to most kids these days.

My grandfather was a bit ruthless about collecting the money. According to Dad's older sister, Pearl, he would even strip search his children to make sure they weren't holding any money back. I think I was fifteen when I went to see my Aunt Pearl at a waitress job. I guess she decided I was old enough to know, so she bragged about being able to keep all her tips, and then let loose with that story. Much to my shock, she added she was my age when this horrifying experience was happening. That's probably why she thought I was old enough to hear the story.

Dad joined the army when he was almost old enough. Like a lot of poor guys, he lied about his age. Grandpa backed him up because he thought my dad would send money home. That only happened when he won at cards. While he was stationed at Fort Bragg, he met my mother.

My mom was in high school and volunteered at the USO. To work in the midst of good-looking men in uniform was a high school girl's dream. She said he would come and stand outside the school, and she would go to the window and sharpen her pencils down to the nubs.

Mom's story is a bit spicier. She says she was three pounds when she was born, and no one expected her to live. They kept her in a little wooden box by the fireplace, to keep her warm. She always said her daddy, Charles, was a bootlegger. He had a big overcoat with pockets inside to carry whiskey.

When she was thirteen, she found out that her mean older sister was really her mother. This meant her parents were actually her grandparents. Her mom, Jeanette, never did tell her who the father was. She sometimes claimed a lady named Lilly as her mom. In later years, Lilly was said to be her grandfather Charles's lady friend. When Lilly left, my mom claims to have spent some time in an orphanage, and then some time in the attic bedroom of a schoolteacher, whose name she never mentioned. When my mom died, I saw a birth certificate that said the last name of her dad was Jackson. Her little brother, Gary, was surprised, since he was always told all five children had the same father, which was not Jackson. He can't confirm anything, because none of them ever met their dad. This would lend to my thinking that my brother Joe had a birth certificate made up for her. Yes, that would be in his wheelhouse to do, as a person considerably lacking in integrity, among other quality attributes.

You may wonder why I use terms that dance around stating anything as fact concerning Mom. It would be because Mom could never tell the truth about anything. She raised my little brother to be the same way. Like all students, he had the potential to surpass the master. Maybe someday I could try to research true facts. Perhaps for my next book, I will spend some time on ancestry. These days, I find discovering the truth about my new bloodline with Father God much more rewarding.

From the outside looking in, our family looked good. We were dressed well enough for middle-class Americans, and we had a nice house and a nice car. My parents were usually pleasant to people. Unfortunately, if you looked behind the curtain, you found something else. Mom had a very violent temper.

At the age of three, I got my favorite dress out of the closet and ran away to grandma's—one house away at the time.

I figured out Mom was too mean to live with. Grandma sent me home again. I decided on the way home there was no one for me in this life. I was on my own to keep myself safe. That was a bit of a self cursing, as it retrofitted me to never let anyone too close.

To Mom, everything was someone else's fault. I could be punished for her breaking a dish. I was often bruised with a belt, a slap, or from a punch on some part of my body. I was not always sure what set her off. Mom once threw the kitchen table at me when I was fifteen. It was a sight, flying through the doorway with enough momentum to take off the molding. I caught it with two hands; even so, it put me on the floor on my back. Still don't know why I was not broken anywhere—grace of God, I guess. At those times, my dad would go throw up and take a nap. I guess he had a weak stomach for it all.

When I was eighteen, I was hunting for my birth certificate to get my driver's license when I found a newspaper clipping that reported my dad was arrested when I was two and a half. Aunt Pearl (Dad's older sister) said it was some mafia thing my dad agreed to take a fall for. He had a big wannabe bad boy streak.

After his arrest, I was immediately sent to a friend's home to live so I would not know what was going on, and so Mom could keep working. Dad actually spent a year in a mental hospital. That apparently was the deal, hospital instead of prison. This was also related to me by Aunt Pearl. I lived with her awhile, then lived with other people and visited my home on occasion through the fourth grade. I remember little of when my dad came home except for the first moment I saw him. I didn't really remember him. It was a scary feeling of, *You're a stranger to me, stuck in my memory,* and I was uncomfortable being pulled up on his lap. Most people were strangers to me then. I felt like I belonged nowhere. That feeling became deeply embedded and tough to wrestle down.

When I was in fifth grade, Mom wanted a house in the country, so they bought one. The next door neighbor became the new fill-in family for my working parents.

They had a daughter my age, Sharon, and we worked at being friends. I was very immature for my age, and my social skills were a little strange. I spent so much time isolated I hardly knew how to have a conversation. In those days, you were to be seen and not heard, in most places anyway. I continually did not fit in anywhere. Down the road from us was another little girl we hung with named Diane. The truth is I tagged along with them, more like they were forced to drag me along. I always had that odd man out feeling. It could have been just my perception, since I had an outsider mindset anyway. As teens, the other two would take each other on little excursions and not include me. I eventually figured out it was because I was too immature for attracting boys' attention. Being attractive to boys is so important to a teenage girl. I didn't have a clue until I was sixteen and we had moved back to the city. It was a real eye opener. City teens have a different mindset than country teens.

In the country, my neighbor took me to a Methodist church. I heard about God there, but with no basis for relationship in me, I really didn't get it. I liked the fun activities, especially the crafty thing. Crafts required little interaction, which I wasn't good at. Choir was good, I didn't have to talk, just sing what everyone else sang. Mom would not go. She gossiped about all the people to me, tearing them apart. So I thought it was all just a good show.

Out there in the country, trees became my comforters. We had a huge old willow tree out in back of our acre. When things got hairy in the house, I would climb to the top of that tree and sprawl out on the branches. My dad was usually the one to come out to look for me. He never found me that I know of. I would like to think it was his way of protecting me. When things seemed quiet, I would slip back inside. Sometimes it worked for me, sometimes not.

The move back to the city for my high school years was a tough adjustment. If I didn't fit in before, I really didn't fit in now.

Mom wouldn't let me do sports after school. She wanted me home, cleaning house and making dinner. I don't think that was the real reason. It more than likely had to do with not wanting to spend the money or time on me. There were obsessive control issues in there, too. I could not even pick out what clothes to wear to school. In my brand of rebellion, I would change my clothes after she left for work. When I got home from school, I would change again.

I learned to be sneaky. I am a lot better these days with being myself in front of people. To overcome this, I keep putting myself out there to talk with people. It can be a little awkward being your authentic self. I am getting better as time goes by. Learning what to share and when to share is still challenging.

This book should help get it all out there.

The first year in the city was OK, but then I began to hang out with some people after school. I would race home and do a fast shuffle to make it look like I did what I was supposed to do. Mom had a surprise baby boy when I was fifteen, named Joseph II. I spent the summer being the babysitter, with promises of being paid. She would come home on payday with a piece of clothing she found in clearance in cellophane bag, and say I bought this or that for you, whether I wanted it or not. Then she wouldn't pay me or pay only a couple of dollars for the week. I learned to never trust her word on anything, because she never could keep it. She could have run for political office with all those empty promises and bald-faced lies.

My dad got me a second job delivering pizza. One job each was not enough for Mom. Having been raised so poor, she always wanted more. I answered phones and took orders. One night, two limos drove up. Men in suits and hats lined a path from the front door to the limo. In walked an old man with a cane, dressed to the nines, ascot and all. He sat in the only booth in a to-go pizza place. I was told to leave the phones and serve him coffee and smile. He asked for cream and sugar, and I put it in for him and stirred the coffee. I obliged everyone. He took one sip and left with the same pomp he'd come in with.

When we all left to go home, Dad asked me if I saw the man who came in with the hat. My brain about exploded "Did I see him?!" but I answered yes calmly, wanting to know why he asked. He said the man wanted to marry me and I should do this because they would be taken care of the rest of their lives. He said it wouldn't be that big a deal because the man was very old and would probably die in six months from having sex with a young woman. I responded calmly, saying it would be my luck he would live longer from having sex with a young woman. Dad did chuckle at that.

Still calm, I said no thank you. The whole conversation was very matter of fact. When you live in a volatile house, you learn to be low-key. Besides, Dad and I hardly ever talked about anything. The only other conversation I can quote is, "Don't make your mom mad." It was a mighty cold week or so at home. I really felt the loss of ground as a child of my parents. I didn't have much as it was. I was not the golden son.

I spent a little time contemplating my value as my parents had just asked their seventeen-year-old virgin daughter to marry an old mafia man and have sex with him. All for their retirement plan. As a virgin, those two things—marriage and sex—just crossed for the first time. It seemed my value was in being a young, voluptuous, red-headed virgin. I believed the best course of action in my adolescent brain was to spoil the goods soon. I found a nice boy to love, so I thought. It took us most of a year to figure out how to spoil the goods. No one explained sex to me until biology that year. He also asked his older brother for instructions. Hey, no laughing at virgins allowed! I was pregnant at graduation. We married, and one day, he came home with a kitten and told me he'd decided to join the navy. Are you kidding me?!

He had a partial scholarship to art school, but because we got married, his parents would not help him go to school. That was sad because he had such an incredible talent at such a young age.

If you will allow me to soap box a little here again. I do think he could have been a great artist if his parents had not abandoned him for marrying me. If they would have helped him go to college, he would have succeeded in his life, even if he eventually divorced me. The navy put him in Vietnam for two tours, where he was exposed to chemical warfare. They gave him a medical discharge. He died at fifty-five, after wandering the streets for thirty years as a paranoid schizophrenic. I plead with all parents to not back out on your child's future success just because they choose to marry. It may or may not work out, but they still need their future. The end!

His diagnosis of schizophrenia didn't come until after years of much violence and abuse occurred.

At one point, I needed to flee for my life and my two children's lives.

I fled from one frying pan to another, and into the fire. I had nothing inside to draw from to make good decisions or have any discernment of good and evil. I lost my way so fast because I was reeling from the trauma of abuse.

There are so many predators out there looking for someone like me to take advantage of. My life right here is a whole other book, one huge mistake after the other. I believed and trusted all the wrong people.

For a while, I lived in a commune in the Hollywood Hills. I thought all was going along nicely. When the Charles Manson stuff hit the news, my house mates began to bail out. It was scary, because we had mutual friends with some of the people there. The other scary part was I was seeing a guy who was going to take me to meet Charles Manson, but my daughter got a toothache that night, so I stayed home. Another God intervention, I believe. After the big killing event, we were all shaken, so we decided it was time to go our separate ways.

I had trouble finding a place I could afford on my own, and called a guy I had worked with in the garment district in the past. He let me stay with him until I could find a place. I discovered after moving in he had other intentions for me. He turned out to be a pimp and a drug dealer. That was my taste of hell.

One night, he decided I needed motivation to be grateful for his help. He threw me into the bedroom. I came to a point where I drew a line in the sand and said no one was going to hit me again. While he was out locking my kids in a room and turning up the stereo to make sure no one heard me scream during my beating, I decided to make a plan to save myself. I got a large knife that was in a drawer, then I unplugged a lamp and stood by the door. When he came in, I was going to hit him on the head, stab him with the knife, then grab the kids and leave.

God intervened again. Suddenly, like the apostle Paul, a blinding light filled the room. I could only look down at the floor. A huge voice called me by name twice. It was not Doris, but I knew it was me. He said "Where is your love now?" Twice. I remember mentally searching myself and coming up empty. It was strange. Then He said, "Turn the other cheek." I said some stupid stuff then: "You don't understand, he is going to beat me. He is going to hurt me." I even swore at Him. "What do you know about pain?" I yelled. Again, He said "Turn the other cheek."

I have no idea why I obeyed that, but it's good I did, because my plan would not have worked well for me. I took the beating. I remember thinking the belt didn't hurt me or break me like when my mom did it. It didn't get to my core. There was something inside me that was different, and I didn't know what it was then. Now I know it was Holy Spirit protecting my soul. The man beat my feet with a coat hanger so I could not run off. The whole point of the beating was to bring me into submission.

To this day, I can hardly believe I had the guts to leave and just pile in my car to head to a place unknown.

We have more options these days for women in crisis. We need so many more. As I have tried to help other women, I have found most of the shelter homes full and poor, especially if they are Jesus centered. I even tried to run one of my own to help broken women. It worked for a few years, but not enough people had empathy for the ministry to fallen women to support it. We started making chocolates. The sales were picking up, but not fast enough, so we could no longer afford to stay open.

The process of learning better started when I asked Jesus into my heart and for the Holy Spirit to help me.

I didn't make any rule keeping or the moral connection right away to God. I have met so many of you out there like that. I am sorry that the Christian community in their zeal tried to do Gods' job and just succeeded in wounding you more. It is not our job to fix you and make you keep rules. You're not a project. Our job is just to love and help until God and you have a relationship He can speak into your issues, and because of that relationship, you would have the power to choose to do differently. He has been the protector of my free will and choices.

I was very much against marriage, because my parents weren't happy. My first marriage didn't work so well, and all subsequent relationships were not so good. I wasn't doing well with the kids, either—no skills.

I signed up to get an early childhood education degree. Silly me, I thought I could do my own self-improvement. This still must have been a God thing. In class, I was learning about all I was lacking. It started me thinking about how I could get new stuff to make a new life. This is part of my come to Jesus story.

After I was saved, I remember going into church feeling like I should marry the guy I was living with, but not wanting to. I said, "God, the only reason to get married would be to have more kids." I always wanted a lot of kids just because I hated being an only child until I was fifteen. With such minimal skills at parenting, I have no idea why I would think I wanted more than the two I was already badly parenting. I did believe a lot of kids needed a real father. I knew the doctor said I could not have more children. I told God, "You will have to let me get pregnant if you want me to marry anybody." Immediately, it felt like a hot water balloon burst inside me, starting at my stomach and radiating out to the top of my head and the tip of my toes and fingers. A very wow experience.

I had a hunch God healed me, but I was only saved a few weeks. I kept that to myself, because people might think me crazy. Does God really answer prayer that fast? In a few weeks, I woke up and craved pickled cauliflower for breakfast. I told my future husband I thought I was pregnant. He was angry because he was told he had too low of a sperm count to have children. He demanded to know who the father was. I told him to stop and think that over. Who is the mother? We didn't use protection, because both of us were sterile. He looked in amazement and said, "Oh yeah!"

"It's God," I said. Well, we got married in our front yard. We put on a potluck picnic in the backyard afterward and took a camping trip to Yosemite. In God's great humor, He gave us twin girls in December.

You may be glad to hear I kept pursuing early childhood education and was a preschool teacher. I got a few skills to work with.

Thank God for miracles. We went from two to four children that year. Interestingly, the twin girls were born on my first son's eighth birthday. It seemed like a do-over times two.

I buckled down and learned to cook and sew and be a real wife and mother. Happily, eventually God put some great ladies in my life to do some show and tell about how love does family.

I learned all my Bible stories from teaching Sunday school to kids. I had to do my homework to teach my class. As I grew more mature in God's way of doing things, I got to teach older kids. I worked an adult prison ministry for a while. I did a lot of high school youth things. Then God asked me to do juvenile detention for a while. I had to leave that to start a women's recovery center. You don't have to know a lot to do this stuff, you just have to be in a relationship where you can hear Papa. Use the God app for that.

When I got my born-again app, I was given a gift of the new nature to grow in me so I could have the same power Jesus did to act out, to manifest that which God had put in me. When you let that process happen, God begins to form His beauty in you and then beauty begins to form around you. What an awesome day it was when my eyes were opened to see the gift of life I had, and it is for anyone who will believe. This was and still is a long process for me. I have had so much to overcome. It has been well worth the pursuit and the struggle. One great motivator is contemplating what my life would be like if I had not pursued this relationship with God. The streets and the news are full of some very sad examples for me.

All through this book, you will find my stories of God helping me. These are my stones of remembrance, the stories that create my apps for that. I am still married to my husband, Steve. I have five beautiful children, and at this point, six beautiful grandchildren and two on the way. God has blessed me with caring friends. I have had the delight of being a part of the God plan to lead many souls to Him. I am blessed to hear Him speak. He has faithfully imparted what I need when I need it. He does things in His time, but He is never too late. I am blessed with a just the right size home for the two of us, cars that run (had plenty that didn't), and knowing He holds the future no matter what life throws at me.

I know He holds yours, too.

Father, from heaven

Help me love your ways
Your stories are adventurous
Your love for me is passionate
Your care for me is merciful
Your provision Is always Faithful
Your ways oh Lord Are Mysterious
Yet, You are always righteous and just
You let my heart break and know your comfort
You let me know affliction and know your healing
You let me know bareness and the treasure
Of your abundance
Your creation speaks loudly, yet you whisper in my ear
You let me hit walls and know your tenderness
You let me know weakness and know your strength
You let me know unworthiness and know your Glory
To know you is better than life
Let your praise Flow continually
From my heart and mouth
Blessed be Your name
My Lord, My God,
My (ABA) Father.

By Doris Bedsole

PROPHETIC

In 1 Corinthians 14:1, Paul says, "Pursue love, and desire spiritual *gifts*, but especially that you may prophecy." He goes on to explain the communication issues in the church. I don't know how you separate plain old hearing God from the prophetic. It has always seemed to me, whenever God has something to say, it carries so much more meaning than I comprehend in that moment. Jesus said in John 10:27 "My sheep know my voice, and I know them. They follow me." (Contemporary English Version) You absolutely need the hearing app, AKA the prophetic.

I am not a Bible school graduate or a theologian. I am just giving you what I would give you if you were at my kitchen table. And the kitchen table just happens to be where I am set up right now to write this chapter.

The prophetic is just hearing from God. If you're a Bible scholar, you can challenge me on that point and probably win, but it fits prophetic for my purposes.

Sometimes you speak it out and sometimes it's just for you in order to help you on your way. No matter what you call it, you need to hear God. You need to practice discerning the way God speaks to you. You need to know God's number and you need to know your own. I think your number is in the account of your strengths and weaknesses. I found it very challenging to be honest with myself about what those are. Trust me here, God will not leave you alone until you are honest with yourself, however long that takes. He is patient and persistent like that.

I have found sometimes, someone will be talking a mile a minute, and I will hear a word or a sentence that rings some bell in my spirit. It will stick with me like cooked spaghetti flung on a wall. I may have to ponder it for a while as God sets more examples before me, or it may come to me quickly. No matter, as time passes, I begin to see that God is trying to communicate a subject to me. He may be trying to create a new mindset.

One of those mindset changing moments came listening to a doctor talk on TV for a few minutes. I could not tell you what he was talking about. But one thing stuck: "You need to act well until you get well." I knew it was God, but I wasn't sure why at the time. I have noticed that if I act as well as possible, I do get well faster. If I have some bug making me ill, I will care for my symptoms and make sure I get extra rest and not exhaust myself. I do recognize my body needs rest and energy to overcome symptoms. My mindset is more my body is having a problem and I will help it, but I, as a person, am not sick. I hope you can grasp what I am trying to say.

You are a three-part person. You have a body, a soul, and a spirit, and they each have different agendas. Your spirit is also a life force that communicates with God and your soul. Your spirit communicates with your soul and your soul with your body. Your soul is your processing center for all incoming information. Your body should work in concert with everything else, and everything else has to work in concert with the body. Have you ever heard anyone say their brain tried to cash a check their body couldn't cover? They planned a vigorous activity in their mind without giving consideration to what their physical body could really do. Soul examination is constantly important to make sure you have not accepted any lies you're working with. The lies lead you to make choices away from God, like Adam and Eve believed the serpent who cast doubt on God's good toward them.

People who struggle with addiction can see the separation of these parts much more clearly because the body cravings have taken the seat of power in their life. It is a tough road to return the power back to where it belongs. The body or soul can be a rebellious child that fights doing what is best for it. They want better for themselves so badly, yet can't seem to get a hold of it.

The transformation that happens in a born-again Christian happens only with this type of open communication. God is creating a new soul within you that has a God's eye view of everything. This is not forced on you, it is *available* to you. God is always guarding and honoring your freedom to choose, because that is what love does. There can be so many wounds in the soul that figuratively speaking, our soul's arms are broken, so it cannot grab hold of the lifeline the spiritual man offers. The strength is within our spiritual man. It can find joy in the Lord, which is your strength. Relationship with a healthier soul is the working principle of an addict's relationship with their sponsor. Like a broken arm needs a splint until it heals, the broken soul needs the relationship of another modeling straight and narrow beside them until they heal.

I remember when I quit smoking. I was up to a pack a day. Trying to quit never worked. One day, I heard the words in my spirit saying, "You don't smoke." It seemed like my key. Every time I wanted to smoke, I repeated the words, "I don't smoke." I actually never smoked a cigarette again. One thing I did eventually notice was that every time I wanted a cigarette, I was on the verge of falling back to my old ways of thinking and doing. A talk with a friend who could remind me of my new truth was my best help.

I look at that experience as practicing thinking well to act well until I got well. I was twenty-six then, and I am sixty-eight now, so I think I can say it worked for me.

I have had many conversations with new Christians who feel like phonies faking their Christianity. It helps to understand the good feeling that can come from doing a right thing doesn't always show up at first; after all, you are going against the person you constructed to protect yourself. He is your previous inner man who you are putting to death. Your new man is actually your authentic self that you put in hiding along the way to self-protect. The new man is the one God created you to be. The new man bears the resemblance of Father God, but with your uniqueness.

I have noticed messages can come in many strange ways. They can be direct thoughts you have in your head. They can come from the radio, TV, something you read, or something you see. No matter how it gets in your spirit, the important thing is to recognize when it is a spirit-filled moment. It is a seed from the realm of heaven planted in you, and it will produce something from that heavenly realm in your life. Remember, seeds are small.

If you feel like a phony, remember that it takes a while for the truth inside of you to take root and become you. It is like digesting food. What you put in your mouth has to go through the digestion process before it becomes a part of your cellular structure and builds up your body, or out it goes.

You are not faking it until you make it; there is no faking in the kingdom. We are a purposed people. Children act like their parents until they mature and become the parent. You are acting well until you get well. You act like your Father until you mature in a matter, and then you will have an understanding of what is actually going on. I wish I had heard that at the beginning of my journey with God. You are purposed to be loved by your Papa God and use that love to love someone else and perpetuate the will of the King of Loving.

It really started before you knew it. You were hearing God the day you accepted Him. Something in your spirit answered His voice, whether you knew it or not. You were created to hear Him. You were created to know Him. In John 17:3, there is a prayer Jesus said out loud, mostly I believe for our benefit. He was being transparent. He said, in essence (I'm paraphrasing), "This is eternal life to know the Father and His son Jesus, the one whom he sent." This knowing is through intimate conversations, at the very least. This open communication is your app for your spiritual upgrade. That is where your smartphone operates. Before you had a smartphone, God was calling you. He called through many different circumstances, and you didn't recognize Him. So many times, you didn't answer. You were too busy with your own thing going on. Still happens occasionally.

My earthly dad had a whistle you could hear for blocks. When I heard it, there was no mistaking it, and I came running home. Nowadays, when Papa God calls, I come because I don't want to miss out on what happens next.

It is always good.

If you didn't know you were called, take a moment to answer your spirit phone now and say hello to a new way of living your life. "Hello, Papa, I want to know you. Papa I want you at the top of my friend circle. Help me to know your voice, to take part in the eternal adventure of knowing you."

The prophetic is not always about foretelling future stuff, it is usually about encouragement. It is love whispering in your ear. It may just be for you because He loves you. It could be for someone else because He loves them. God knows we need confirmation from outside our head sometimes. He will do that too. He will bring someone else into the process to let you know you're on the right track. He also wants us to be in concert with others in our new family life. We need to experience the fact that we are not alone.

The prophetic is what you need to hear right now, your link to the Trinity, your Father God, your brother Jesus, and Holy Spirit. It is your smartphone.

Yes, Jesus is your brother. He is the first born of the children of God. It is in the Bible (Romans 8:29). This means you number among the children of God. When you are born-again, you become an eternal being. Jesus is in heavenly places with the transfigured body. You will get one too when your time comes. For now, you are on this leg of your spiritual eternal journey.

It is a process to learn to discern God's voice, just like it is a process to learn to use your iPhone or Android phone.

I have had my Android two years and still don't get half of what it can do for me. Learning this is like anything else, trial and error. Be patient with yourself and others, you will get it. Don't give up—never give up.

My husband and I once made a bad investment. We prayed about what to do, and waited, and prayed, and waited. We heard nothing. In my human reasoning, I decided God didn't say no, so let's do it. Hubby thought that too. We desperately need a retirement fund, and we were a wee bit greedy enough to take a risk for a large profit. Well, we were taken for a large chunk of change on that one, along with many other people. Lesson here for me is, if you don't hear, don't do it! Hearing nothing is apparently equivalent to NO. It sure wasn't a yes, God would not do that to us. Write that down.

By now, you are probably noticing that I use so many word pictures. God and I communicate well this way. I once asked Him why. He said, "I need to create frames of reference for you to understand me." I like that about God. He knows me and what helps me understand Him. There are so many ways God uses to communicate with us. I talk with my friends about how they hear God. So far, no one is saying they have only one way they hear. One friend kept seeing the numbers 111 everywhere. She kept watching and waiting for an explanation. Eventually, she heard a speaker quote a scripture that had those numbers for a Bible reference. There was a family situation in her life at that time, and she needed to hear that word right then; it just took her almost a year to come to meet the moment it was needed. God prepared her to not let the moment pass without notice. You'd better believe it was life changing.

Another friend got a word stuck in her mind, so she looked it up in the dictionary; the word ministered to her situation, bringing much needed clarity.

Some just suddenly know the problem another person is struggling with and ask if it is true. (Some circles call this reading someone's mail.) Usually it is, and then the Holy Spirit gives the words to them to speak to the situation. These happen to me too. Most of the time, I get a picture and an understanding starts to open itself to my mind. And I just think, wow, I've never thought like this before. I wouldn't think like that. But God does. LOL.

It is important to note here that there is a difference between this kind of prophetic and the office of the prophetic. These are two different things. God does appoint certain people to prophesy to the church at large, and it is usually not the one going around touting "I am a prophet."

It is usually apparent that someone is something by the way they act, not because they say so. I can usually tell someone is a teacher because they are instruction oriented in their relationships, too. It should get obvious to you what a person's role is without them advertising it.

The everyday hearing from God is what is needed so much everywhere these days. In the times we live in, God is not making many new spiritual superstars like Katherine Kuhlman and Billy Graham. The reason is He is calling all His people to maturity and to step up. He is pouring out His Spirit on all flesh. That means you and me, and I am excited about that. This is the season of the ordinary person getting to stand in the Glory of God. In case you wondered, you don't bring God Glory, God lets you stand in His, and you get to enjoy the light.

The prophetic app makes you interactive with the God who created the universe. He desires to be alive and well and active in you. He desires you to do exploits with Him. No worries, He has made all the arrangements and has all the details covered. You just have to answer your call and listen. Then agree and wait for your cue.

Remember, the prerequisite to this is to enter the love relationship with Papa God and be born-again. You need His Spirit in you because spiritual things are spiritually discerned. Meaning the organic brain will not get it. You can't be smarter than God. Your spirit gets the message, then communicates it to the soul; the soul alerts the parts of you that need it, and the body responds. Be careful, as you know a lot can get lost in translation. Most of us have played the party game where you pass a message from one person to the next and at the end, it comes out completely different. It can happen internally too.

Receiving and recognizing your prophetic gift enables you to work much better in concert with God, others, and, oh yeah, yourself. Remember you are made up of three parts, and sometime we put the wrong part at the head.

The prophetic can be a gesture to someone when you don't really understand your compulsion to do it. Often, your understanding comes after the fact. If you have ever shown up at the right place at the right time, you know that divine providence set that up. That can be considered a prophetic moment too. Last night, I was drawn to hug a young woman at a meeting. I did not know how much she needed a mother's love when I did it. I did not know her story. I felt her totally relax and surrender to God's love for her. It was a prophetic act I was privileged to be part of.

I saw a teenager be moved to draw a circle on a piece of paper and hand it to someone they didn't know. He told them God said stand on it and you will get healed. He didn't even know they needed healing, yet they were healed. This beautiful teenager's phone was on, and he answered the call and owned up to his cue.

My friend was at a bus stop and God said, "Someone with an orange sock will be here; tell her I love her and I care." A girl with one giant orange sock came around the corner. She had injured her foot and had a medical sock on it. My friend delivered the message and the girl was healed as she hobbled, then walked, away. How fun was that!

Once, I was packing my suitcase for a high school youth retreat. My husband teased me for throwing odd stuff in my suitcase that I would not need. I felt unexplainably pressed to do it. A few hours into the retreat, these items were desperately needed. What if I had agreed with the person teasing me and dismissed those thoughts? I got to stand in God's Glory of provision for some of God children. It was a privilege, and way more fun.

One Christmas, when we'd first moved to El Toro, California, there were two sheets of plywood left in the garage by previous occupants. One day, walking through the garage, I looked at the plywood and got the notion I should cut out four-foot figures for a nativity. I was obsessed with getting it cut out and painted. I stayed up all night to finish it so I could put them up out in front of our house. They were adorable. They looked like big-eyed preschoolers dressed like the nativity. I did not know I had that in me. A couple of weeks went by, and there was a knock on my door. My neighbor across the street stood sheepishly at my doorstep. She began to tell me that her three-year-old asked her every day when they went out, "Who are the people in the pictures?" Every day she would tell him, "Jesus, Mary, and Joseph." That day, when she gave him the same answer, he'd said, "Mommy, why every time I ask you who it is, you swear?" She said she realized she never told him anything about God and she had better start. She decided she should not use those words as swear words, either. I smiled and hugged her. My wood pictures did their job. I got to stand in God's Glory again. Way cool and fun.

To me, that was a prophetic act and I will never forget it. It so impressed on me to not ignore the call of God, even if it's just a silly idea in my head I don't believe I have the talent for. You can feel impressed to do a lot of different small acts of kindness that you think are silly or insignificant. Do them; it is your phone ringing, answer up.

When God addressed me in a worship service to talk to the people about upgrading their communication skill and being like a smartphone, I had no clue it would lead to writing this book. At this point, I have no idea what will happen next. I am loving this adventure, so whatever is OK with me.

I have a hope it will demystify a relationship with God to people who look from the outside in. For that to happen, God has to get someone to read it. I am happy you are.

LOVE OF GOD

God is love, (1 John 4:16), and true love comes from God.

Your love for God comes from God. Kind of like your kids using their allowance to buy you a present. Because He first loved us (1 John 4:10) Jesus is our app to Papa. He already took the first step and so much more; it is our turn to respond.

He made you and He loves His creation. He loves to demonstrate His love.

Relationship is part of love, in case you hadn't noticed. I am so grateful He knows how to do relationship, because I don't do it so well. I have spent way too much time in self-preservation because of my upbringing. I have been noticing among the people I know, most of us come from families who are dysfunctional to some degree or another. Self-preservation doesn't spend a lot of time on connecting or seeing about the needs of others. It is very busy securing its own needs and protecting the walls it has constructed. The unhealed soul does not want its wounds messed with.

His patience and forgiveness is part of His love. The world and all that is in it was created to express the love inside the Trinity. Jesus is a demonstration of His love. He is the Word (kind of the essence of God) made in human form. Jesus was the firstborn of the children of God. We have been invited into the community of love with the Father, Son, and Holy Ghost. When we accept His offer, we are counted among the children. I could be His two billion, two hundred and forty-seventh daughter. His family is very big.

It is His kindness that leads us to repentance (Romans 2:4). His kindness, mercy, and graces are new every morning. Every day, we have a new chance at everything. That is a love I love to love.

Worldly love is so unkind to us because of our shortcomings. It sometimes seems the people around us are self-appointed floggers for our imperfections. You may think yourself to be a patient and kind person. To you I would say kudos for practicing an attribute of God. No doubt it has brought you many blessings. I still hold to the belief, if real love exists in your life, it is from God; it is His app for you whether or not you attribute it to him, believe in Him, or not. He is always in pursuit of a love relationship with you, and He is relentless.

I once heard Dean Braxton talk about his experience of dying, going to heaven, and coming back. I love to hear those kinds of stories. He said when he met Jesus, he fell at his feet and stared at them. He could hardly believe how much love there was for him emanating just from Jesus's feet. He said it was as if he were the only child in existence and had His total focus of love and attention. Dean or I don't know how God could do that, but we are so glad He does. How can you not return love to someone who loves you like that? For me, it is greater than anything I have experienced on earth.

If you're having trouble with receiving so much love coming at you, let me tell you, you're not alone. God had come to me many times, but I was not open to it nor did I recognize my need for what He was offering. Most of us won't. I just wanted fixes for my situations. I recognized one day, by the grace of God, I was empty inside. I finally was open to looking for a better answer. I started to search for what was causing me so much pain and grief internally. I tried to fill the hole with everything the world had to offer, and I was still stuck. Why did nothing work? Why could I not make myself feel better? Why did the answers the world offered not work for me?

Counseling could draw a circle around it and make it a large target for the enemy of my soul, but offered insufficient help to fix it.

I needed Jesus and to know God's love, a love like no other. It was the only real remedy to heal the cavern of my soul's pain and begin to heal the damage done to the child who was shuffled around for other people to care for. I needed healing from the harsh rule of a mom who could only act out of the pain inside her, too, and a father who was so very distant and unapproachable.

I had an awesome salvation experience of being loved for the first time. I knew it to be true and still had a hard time accepting I was loved by God, even though I knew it was real in my head and had great feelings at that moment. The problem was me, not God. I didn't love me. I believed no one had ever loved me. I had no grid to put love in. I had so much trouble accepting the new identity as a beloved child of the King. I was born-again, and a new creature was spiritually born on the inside, but I was still carrying around the old, dead, unlovely me. The unlovable me was the lie I created in response to my childhood. I believed more in the lie of the manufactured me than I believed in the true me God was creating.

I tried to be a chameleon. I dressed like a Christian and copied some of their words for a while. It was obvious to me and I am sure others, too. I was trying to act well until I could get well. I sometimes think God lets us do our thing at trying to make ourselves right. I think when we surrender in frustration from seeing it not working, He can finally step in and lead us because we answer our phones and are receptive to relationship and directions. One lie that can keep you from receiving your call is thinking you have to fix yourself before you are acceptable to the relationship. Stop trying to create a form of godliness. You and God are one of a kind together. He will do it with you. You can't do it without Him. The material for the new reborn you comes out of the heaven of the Trinity.

One day, God said to look in the mirror. "Look yourself in the eye and tell yourself 'I love you.'" Oh my, that was painful. I could hardly look myself in the eye to start with. I never realized a person could look at themselves and never really see themselves. These little sessions kept going for a long time. They went from "I love you" to "God loves you, and I love you." Then He hit me with, "God loves you, and I love you, and I will take care of you and keep you safe." I still do one of those sessions from time to time. I want to make sure I don't lose any ground. It is amazing how assured the soul gets after a spirited affirmation session. God and I have added many declarations to myself these days. I am worthy. I am acceptable and accepted. I am brave enough to be writing a book God commissioned. I dance in worship to God because He said He would deliver his children from their bondages if I would dance. God has an answer for every issue I face. No worries, be joyful. That names a few. I assure you I am still human and very flawed, with days I have to drag myself to prayer. Papa is so much more compassionate than I, with my less than lovely attitudes and forgetfulness of His love and goodness toward me.

The time in front of the mirror was and still is well spent. Something eventually happened inside me. It was like a big door began to open so I could know God, and His love started pouring into me. I think that was my app for that. I could finally start to believe I was loved. I saw myself differently. I could see more clearly and understood my past actions. I was covering my past instead of revealing my future. I can't fix my past. I had to realize that the blood of Jesus paid for it all. It belongs to Him now to do with as He chooses. I am thinking He is choosing this book to help me get a correct perspective of what is behind so I can do a better job of going forward. My response right now to His love is to write about it. I have no idea at this point what He will do with it. I do know that writing it is building a whole new part of me. It is the least I can do to show my gratitude for His love in my life. Scripture says the wages, the earned result, of sin, choosing my own way, is death. Jesus stepped in and gathered all the wages from Adam and Eve, through the end of earth time, into Himself so we could be free. So we could be born-again into a spirit-filled life.

I think I would be remiss if I didn't clarify something here—I did have to do some past work. I spent some sessions with a few wonderful people who helped me to work through my stuff. I expound on that in the healing and wholeness chapter.

I have observed we humans seem to accept this PAID IN FULL truth in increments. The Bible keeps saying things like **all** sin, **all** provision, and **all** people **all** the time. We seem to think in parts. Today this much only is covered in the payment. Then maybe later, we will add a little more. My personal twist was God can save or change everyone but me or the one person who is giving me the most grief. He can't save or change them. I am impossible for God. They are impossible for God. The truth is nothing is impossible for God, and nothing is left out of God's **ALL**. Luke 18:27. Amen.

Once you understand fully what the love of God is, you will realize it is filled with so much mercy and grace, not just truth and rules. Any rule you see is for your greatest good. Then you get sin, which is always in the opposite direction from your greatest good. However, He always leaves you with the freedom of choice.

When you don't feel like you have a choice, you might be participating in something going in the opposite direction from God. If you feel like you can't stop something (loss of freedom) like a harmful addiction, it's time to check yourself.

Can you see the stark contrast of sin life to a love life? It can be like turning on the lights after being in the dark a long time, or even in the grays. Things begin to be discernible. You start to understand why you need Jesus and what you were saved from and for. I choose the love life. Scripture says every moment, we have a choice between life and death. Choose life.

The way I see it, God is in me, so I have love, and because His love is active, I am doing my best to let His love take action through me. At least as much action as I can comprehend. I used to say I did some things because it was the right thing to do. I am seeing now that I do more things because they are the *loving* things to do. The same scenario applies to things I won't do. I don't hit you with a baseball bat because it would hurt you. Even though that is true, I don't hit you with a bat because it would not be a loving thing to do. A snowball, maybe.

One thing I would like to add is God loves creativity. He is a creator and He loves to see His kids create. I love the fact I found a church that lets me express my creative love in dance. We have people painting pictures in places during our worship. The Spirit of God speaks and moves through all creative expressions. He loves in so many different ways. You are one of His expressions of love. In the book *The Shack*, by Wm. Paul Young, there is a line that says, "He is especially fond of you."

I really want to thank you, Baxter Kruger, for saying "God always wanted a child just like you." That word means so much to the child's heart in me who thought she was not wanted.

Thank you, Papa God. You always wanted me. I always want you.

THE FRAGRANCE OF LOVE!

Devine love has come to us
It has walked and Talked to us
It has left its potent fragrance
Whirling like a merry dance
With a path of Sorrow and glee
Adventure created just For you and me.
What is this fragrance That woos me?
Lingering, it intoxicates Me with liberty
Yet, it stirs A burning desire
To be in its grip
It holds me so steadfast I know I won't slip
My love bears gifts Of presence, time
And gentleness
Rapturing my heart
With a sweet
Truth kiss

By: Doris Bedsole

LOVE FOR OTHERS

The Holy Spirit, when it moves into you, sheds the love of God abroad in our hearts for <u>all</u> men (Romans 5:5). The first person you have to figure out how to love is yourself. The great commandment was to love your God with all your heart, mind, soul, and strength. Love your brother as <u>yourself,</u> and on this hinges all the laws of the prophets (Matthew 22:37).

One of the first lies the enemy will tell you is that to love yourself would be conceited and proud. Those are completely different traits from love. Walking this road awhile, I am finally getting it. My life was a gift from the love of God. If God gifted me with a Rolls Royce, I would take care of my precious gift. I would give it the right gas and oil, keep it clean, be careful how I drove. Just because I did good things for my car does not mean I am conceited or proud. Why would I not want to take good care of my gift and make the best of it? I always want to share the gifts He gives me. This book is sharing way more than I ever thought I would.

Some of us have trouble with the self part, and that is why we have trouble loving others. They are not like us, so we just don't get them. We don't have to get them to love them, just be respectful and kind. They don't have to get us to love us, or be respectful and kind back. God gets all of us, and can love them all through us one way or another, if you choose to set yourself on that course.

Most of us haven't figured out the love yourself part. All real love comes from God. I am not talking about an affection that attaches us to something. Many of us think we love ourselves, but what we really are doing is making ourselves comfortable with superficial padding. We make ourselves comfort addicts. We go for the bigger chairs, bigger TVs, better cars, better clothes—we are very subtle with what we do. Spoiling yourself to ruin is not self-love. That would be called self-indulgence. We all become self-centered for too much of our life, but it is not love. You and I have covered much of this in previous chapters. Our maturity should eventually lead us to a paradigm shift of thinking of others. Unfortunately, some of us had an upbringing that put us in self-protect mode, building walls to keep others at a safe distance. All the while, we were really building our own prison around us. As we work on getting our soul wounds healed, we will better discern who to let into our circles and when.

No parent who spoils a child will like the outcome. If you are like me, I had to study up on good parenting. I didn't have the example set before me growing up. My daughter, Bridgette, has become the parent I always wanted to be. She once gave me the *Parent Effectiveness Training* book she used for a class she took in college. I think that was a subtle clue about something. Now she is spreading the new wisdom of the Love and Logic book to all who will listen.

In the previous chapter on the love of God, I told you about my mirror sessions. That was a great lesson for growing wholeness and wellness in my life. This process in front of the mirror helped me to heal by pressing the truth into the core of my believer. Making the commitment to let God love me, and to love and care for myself, took me out of my victim mindset. This shift in thinking was a whole new world for me. When I loved myself, I could then love others like I loved myself. I learned to make boundaries for myself and respect them. I used to think other people would be hurting me just because they kept their boundaries. Now I see and am experiencing the peace that comes with boundaries. These were defining lines of God at work in me, making me who He called me to be. Boundaries are not walls to keep people out, they are markers that help people live peacefully and respectfully with each other. You can ask permission to cross boundaries. It does make life pleasant.

When I received the Spirit of God and healing began, I could see people more from His perspective. It is no longer about what I think of them or feel toward them based on a mutated picture of myself or them. I have mentioned we all have a grid of our collected information and experiences. We look through this perspective and try to interpret everything in those little grid boxes of our understanding. So much of what God and others are doing is not interpreted correctly. We are trying to make it fit into our own understanding. News flash: it won't.

Here comes the next huge paradigm shift of perspective in my grid. My interest in myself and other people began to come from God's point of view and not just mine. The thought that is always in the front of my mind is, "What does God want for them and for me in this moment and in this situation?" I am now in His family and on His team. I recognize I am an ambassador of the kingdom of God. The kingdoms' interest has to do with all of us as family.

God is a Trinity of Father, Son, and Holy Spirit. They deeply love each other. This is important, because if there was just God the Father, then everything would be just about Him and that would make Him narcissistic. They are three persons, and we have been invited into this circle (a culture) of love, honor, and blessing. It may not seem like it at first, but it is the truth. I had to get to a place of understanding that the problem with me was not God's fault, it was that my perspective of Him was not true.

This new life is not about you or me acting perfectly for this world or for a religious standard. I am discovering the perfect one who is already in me. In this relationship, I am becoming like the one I am spending my time with. Because His Spirit is in me, He births His own character in me. I don't have to get love, mercy, grace, or forgiveness outside myself. I have it already, and I have it in abundance. I just need to call it up on my smartphone. When you think about it this way, it can seem like we have more of an intercom than a smartphone. That might be another book. I have access to all God has intended for me to have at this time. If I want more, I go and find out if this is the pursuit I am supposed to be on at this time.

This place of acceptance, love, and peace I come from is my relationship with Him. The only desire I am really pursuing is to know more of the Jesus I am in relationship with, who provided all this for me. Then I follow His lead on giving it away. I know it sounds oversimplified. The problem I have is sometimes tripping over myself—I do get in my own way.

I have spent much time pondering why that is. When I get into trouble, I sit down and have a pow-wow with myself. I have to ask myself, *How did I get here?* This talk with self really helps. Of course, I am not isolated in this conversation; the Trinity is always there. I make that call and employ my app for that.

We are three-part beings: spirit, soul, and body. My trouble starts when I am in discord. If I got the three parts of myself to come into agreement with each other and with God before I opened my mouth, I would do better. My looking in the mirror exercise helps a great deal to bring my three parts in harmony with myself.

It helps to identify your parts. The body wants one thing, the wounded soul is protecting itself, operating in fear, and the spirit wants to go another direction. If you know how each part operates, you can identify it in yourself and in others. You or others could be talking from intellect, a wounded soul, or from spirit. Knowing which part of someone or yourself the statements are coming from helps you decide the best response for you and them.

It is easier to represent the generosity of heaven with its wisdom, kindnesses, mercy, and hospitality as you get more at one with yourself and with God. We need to get on the same agenda. When I am correctly demonstrating Him, He backs me up. I can now give out of the God of the universe who owns the cattle on a thousand hills, not out of my small pocket. I can love with a greater love than my little heart.

As I found my true authentic self, this new me began to manifest the gifts of the Holy Spirit. Not the self that was manufactured in response to the world around me, with its unrealistic rules and measuring sticks. I am growing in response to God's love and acceptance of me. These eyes now see better His care for me and others. I am seeing and have more empathy for the plight of others who are struggling between the real self and the manufactured self. The struggle in this life seems not be not so much with evil as it is with mindsets and in making the transition of leaving the old ways and lies behind.

We were not asked to save people. The Spirit of God does that. We were asked to make disciples, heal the sick, and set the captive free. You can only do that by loving people with God's love. Remember, it is His kindness that leads to repentance.

There are so many aspects of the goodness of God that escaped me when I walked in darkness. Being now in His light, I can open my heart and shine His light to the world. Jesus is light, and He is in me. So many walk about dark minded, not seeing good anywhere. Isaiah 60:1 says, "Arise, shine; For your light has come!" It was a word of hope for Israel while they were still in captivity to slavery, and it is a word of hope for us.

I saw a special miracle happen in me when I gave all the pain of life to Him. He said he has made me a jewel. Every pain and suffering became a facet in the master jewel cutter's hand. The thing about jewels is the more facets, the more refracted light there is. That means it sparkles for all to see the beauty. I would be the beauty of the Lord.

He does come bearing gifts. Wise men still seek Him, and so do I. I know I have not arrived. I am still a work in progress, and God has much to do in me. Like the truth about love, I am still working it all into my belief system.

My grappling hook firmly planted, I am in process, like everyone else growing in grace.

Lately, I am feeling more like the revelations God gives of His truth are Him planting the hook deeper in me and pulling me closer and closer to it and to Him.

When the truth finally hits my core belief system, I think the power I want to see will be activated in me. I am hungry to see those signs and wonders following me.

It was natural to me to want to bring what I was learning about God to my family of origin. I moved to New York because my dad was ill in 1973, and I thought it important I spent time with him before he died. I left home at nineteen, and now I was thirty-two. I thought I could repair old wounds and finally have family. It was a hard lesson for me to learn that you can't make other people heal relationally or any other way if they don't want to. Some people can be so entrenched in their stuff, they can't let go and see there is a better way. God respects our free will, even if it kills us. Many perish for lack of knowledge; it is in Hosea 4:6. I do have the satisfaction of knowing I tried. I have learned you can't care more about a person than they care about themselves. It is very easy to slip over to making the result more important than the person and the relationship. When you start to make choices for people rationalizing that it's in their "best interest," they lose their free will. Then you have tried to make yourself their god. That is not the job I want.

I have noticed, and I am sure you have too, that the people we think should act better just don't. One day, I complained to God about my fellow Christians. He gives such interesting responses to my complaints. He said the earth church is like a theater stage production. When an actor forgets their lines, falls down, or just stands in the wrong place, the actors don't stop right there, point out, and discuss what is wrong or vote you off the stage. In a performance, they keep on going and act past whatever happened. They begin to alter their lines and actions to work it in so that the audience hardly notices what happened. The audience in our case is the world watching how we deal with issues. It is how we fellow Christians are supposed to act instead of always pointing stuff out about others. Why do we labor so much at exploiting others' mistakes and trying to fix them? That is God's job, not ours. If they are open to truth or want help, then give some. I can't make people better; I can't even make myself better. My best happens when I spend time getting in agreement with God. There is a scripture that says love covers a multitude of sins. It must be what real mature love does. I can always count on God to put things in perspective for me.

My life translation of this uses the example of my craft projects. My friends and I often make mistakes or something happens in the projects we are working on. We have learned to create around and over whatever happened and call it a custom design element. Many wonderful new creations have been born this way. In a way, I think that is what God does with us. Whatever mistakes we made, He works it in as a custom design element, making all things work together for the good of those who love Him.

I get these movies from God from time to time in my sanctified imagination. It is like an internal movie screen. I don't know any other way to describe it. I have learned to just roll with it, then stop and ponder them, because they are just full with messages.

One day, this particular movie started while I was doing dishes in my kitchen. In this movie, Jesus was at the front door, and He had a refrigerator on a dolly. I opened the door for him and he came in. Then I went immediately to the back door and opened it so I could move it out and give it away. He said, "No, this is for you, and I have more." I was very puzzled, because I have always had the mindset of whatever God gives me, I give it away. My natural mind was also telling me at the time that my house was full of furnishings.

Then he gave this instruction: "You can't give what you don't have." I looked around my house in the vision and saw, to my surprise, it was empty. He said, "How will you feed them when I send them if you have no place to keep the food I give you. How will you serve them without my table or chairs? How will you comfort them without my couch? How will you give rest without my bed?" Suddenly, it became clear He wanted to install things in my life that would serve others from Him. Then I could give more in a different way. I needed to have His spiritual food, His table and chairs, His couch with His kind of comfort, His bed of EVERLASTING ARMS resting me. It was getting clearer that I had a new level of learning before me. What the world had furnished me with was not what God wanted me to give. His kind of everything is different. I think that is another book, too. I am still working that one out.

Tommy Barnet once said, "If it doesn't work at home, don't export it." I have seen many ministries fail trying to serve a religion and not God, out of their own good will to prove they were godly. It is so important to know you are doing something with God and not trying to get God to do something with you. Love with God and love with family need to be in place before you can love outside the front door to any meaningfully significant degree. If it's not inside, if you haven't let God install His home in you and a throne in you, then you are not working out of a right relationship. If you haven't let Him install His throne, you won't have much power either. My life needed to be a living example of what the presence of God is in order to represent well. Reality check: I am still working on it.

Please don't think I am saying you have to be perfect to be used by God effectively. We will always be in process. The level of our effectiveness is in proportion to our letting the process happen in us. Every piece God gives is valuable and viable; you do not have to have all the pieces together to have something to give away. Rest in this fact: He is the all sufficient God who can do a lot with even a little. Take for example feeding 5,000 people with a few loaves of bread and fish. Working with Him is the fastest route to knowing Him outside of worshiping and soaking in His presence. I have decided everything I do is worship to Him anyway. I am blessed to just be alive and part of this adventure, so anything that happens now is grace letting me stand in His Glory.

Not so long ago in worship, I had one of these visions of God coming as a lion and sitting in front of the sanctuary. I have seen the movie *The Lion, the Witch and the Wardrobe*. Very creative way C.S. Lewis represented the God story as the Lion of Judah. I never related to that side of God's personality. In the church service, I kept waiting for him to roar, but He didn't until the visiting preacher (Dean Braxton) began to speak. Then He said, "Now I am

90

roaring, and one day you will roar for me too." Since I belong to a Prophetic Art group that meets Monday nights, the next day, I attempted to draw a lion face. When I started my picture, in a vision, this lion came and stood beside me. He came with a strong, overwhelming presence I could see in the spirit and feel with my body, too. I felt such a strong love emanating from Him, tears began to run down my face. I could hardly keep going. I left the table and went to another room on the floor. That is when He came again as the lion, and I began an interactive experience with the lion, rolling on the floor with Him and pressing into His furry mane. I have never experienced such love, acceptance, and friendship. There was close bonding happening that had never happened before. I could hardly believe He was that playful and lovable. I was weeping, smiling, and feeling such comfort and trust in this closeness. It was really beyond words, and very outside my grid. I asked myself, *Why am I not afraid of a lion? A lion is a wild jungle animal. He is not a tamable house pet. You cannot tame God.*

Is this why religions try to keep Him in a box? Is this why we as a people keep Him at what we think is a safe distance from our lives? I knew I could trust this lion not to hurt me, because I knew Him as one who had a plan for my welfare and not my destruction. He was not tamed to do what I wanted, but He was a trusted one who would not attack and hurt me. I remembered in the story that they spoke of the lion Asland as friendly but not safe. I can only think they were talking about His adventurous spirit. Perhaps it means our selfishness and our walls are not safe around him.

I think I can carry this over into my love for others app. You too are a bit wild like me, like him. I have my terms of endearment, so do you. It seems every encounter is a negotiation of relationship terms between you, me, and God. I can respect your boundaries and you can respect mine, but we both need to bow to God's. We continue to love in the ways we can in hope of being able to dwell in the kingdom together. If we are both laboring to agree with God, eventually we will have common ground.

I have read a lot lately about inner healing from many kinds of abuse. The authors all talk about addressing your wounded part and letting Jesus in to heal it. The other part they all agree on is we need to find a replacement for the one who wounded us. For me, it was the harsh mother and the emotionally absent father. I can forgive them, but I also need to find a woman in the family of God who can show me a mother who is kind and understanding. I needed to find a father figure to see what a good dad was like. Once I see it in action, I know that is how God is toward me and then He can begin to heal those wounds. We need each other. You don't know who in the family needs that piece of God you have. And they might have a piece you need. We are all flawed and wounded. We will only heal when we let God be active in us and touch other people's lives.

Risk it, get out there and love on people.

They desperately need it. So do you.

WISDOM

The dictionary defines wisdom as the ability to discern inner qualities and relationships, having insight, good sense and judgment, a wise attitude or course of action, and being prudent in all your ways.

The Bible states that wisdom begins with fear of the Lord. It is a fear that refers to respect. It is the kind of respect that is about you knowing the power of something, so you treat it with regard to its potential for good or bad. This brings to mind high-voltage electricity.

My daughter's husband once thought he could fix their simple electrical problem in the attic without turning off the breaker. Suddenly, she heard him flopping about in the tiny attic and promptly stuck herself through the access hole and yanked his leg hard enough to pull him away from the wire. He now has a great deal more respect (fear) for electricity. You take certain precautions and have much more thought before you handle it, because it can kill you. The same respect would go for fire because it can hurt, kill, and destroy when not contained or handled properly.

I became a campfire girl at ten, thanks to my next door neighbors. Neighbors are a gift from God to the children they take under their wings. My next door neighbor invited me to church and campfire girls with them. Both of these things helped give me information and experience I would one day need. Most kids have had talks with their parents about the facts of life at least. My parents were not big on talking to me about much of anything, so I was very naïve about many things. I guess passing on wisdom never occurred to my parents, or they just didn't think it important to share. Looking back at my parents' history, they didn't have that much to share. They were raised in fear and intimidation, so that was their parenting style. I must credit them with teaching me a work ethic and not being afraid of hard work.

My first mishap with heat was my first camp-out with the campfire girls. We made tinfoil dinners and placed them on the fire. I got very impatient to get mine out. How hot is hot? How hot does fire make everything around it? That should have crossed my mind. I plucked it out with my bare hands. *Scream*! Does burning hot only pertain to fire? I learned to iron at twelve. While my parents were at work, I had chores to do. One of my keep the kid busy chores was ironing the towels, sheets, and pillowcases. I decided to try ironing a pleated skirt. I was having difficulty, so I threw my leg over the ironing board to help me hold it. I was not such a careful twelve-year-old, so in my haste, I pushed the iron into my leg. *Scream*! With no one else at home, I attempted to doctor myself. I then proceeded to go outside and distract myself from the pain. I bet you think that was a good idea. My mom came home from work a few hours later, and when she went in the house there was another scream. It was my name. I went in knowing I was in trouble, but with no idea what for. Apparently, I forgot to turn the iron off, and the iron burned out, leaving two large melted metal drips on the bottom of the iron on its way out. Yes, Mother was angry.

I never did tell her about my leg burn. I took my lashes and went to my room. I learned to stay out of an angry mother's way. I have many more episodes I could tax you with, having to do with cooking, curling irons, even more with ironing my hair as a teen. I think I was the original fry baby. I did smarten up eventually. Truly, this wisdom was born of pain. I was the kid I am sure people laughed about. God healed me enough so I can look back and laugh at my dumb behavior. I think remembering these things gives me more patience with other people's behavior.

A word to parents: Do not let your kid grow up like a vacant lot full of weeds and trash. Weeds and trash are what form when nothing is planted. You make sure they are a garden of delight; plant in them as much beauty and wise fruit as you possibly can. Share your life and wisdom generously with them. They learn processes from watching you work through your problems and overcome failures. I have learned failure only happens when you give up.

I have found God to be kind and loving and very much desiring relationship. Like any good parent or tender lover, I have found Him eager to share His wisdom with me, if I would just ask. Oh, sitting still long enough to hear it helps too.

In this relationship, I can appreciate the value of this great grace, mercy, and care so much more, since I know without Him I earned death and destruction for my self-centered and destructive ways. The one who loves me so much has the power to do this.

How fortunate are we, and me particularly, that He chooses love, grace, and mercy. Sometimes when we are paying our consequences for our choices, it is hard to remember. He is drawing us to Himself the easiest way we will come. He did set up a universe to administer correction and blessing. We have all heard the golden rule of doing unto others as you would have them do unto you. That is handy, because it does come back to you. What goes around comes around. Life is a school and a wise person pays heed to its lessons. I have noticed the longer you make excuses for yourself and don't learn your lesson, the consequences get harder and harder.

Solomon was considered the wisest man in his time. During his wisest times, he wrote the Proverbs. A lot of foolishness and pain can be avoided by paying attention to them. I lost count of how many times I read them, trying to absorb them into my being. I came into this relationship with Him realizing I was almost as dumb as a post.

Solomon also wrote Ecclesiastes after he did not follow his own wise advice. It is how he figured out what he wrote about. Vanity, vanity, all is vanity; sounds like a guy who overindulged in life. He was rich enough to follow every avenue of life to its bitter end and find it empty. Sometimes our mistakes are our best teachers. It is wisdom to look at mistakes that way, then move on with the wisdom and knowledge we have gained. Now I am so very careful around hot stuff. LOL.

In my mind, I have defined my relationship with God as awe, wonder, and reverence for a love like no other. I am defining this fear as reverence. I truly want this God and His wisdom to stay in my life. When you eagerly participate in a relationship and want to keep the expressions of love going, that is not fear to me. It is a manifestation of a healthy relationship in action.

I have seen many people who are book smart and life foolish, lacking in what I would call common sense and even human wisdom. Common sense can be great up to a point. When it comes to spiritual things, the wisdom of God often makes little sense. I learned from Oswald Chambers that if common sense was all we needed, God would not have needed a book or to ever speak. We would not have needed Jesus to come and then send us a Holy Spirit to counsel and empower us. He also said to be on guard to never let common sense override your spiritual sense. Whatever comes from heaven will always work out better.

God comes at interesting times to instruct in His wisdom. I have spent way too much time unhappy with my life. Once while working on my roses, God took time to speak to my heart. He said life can be like roses; they are beautiful, but they come with thorns. You have to take precautions to handle them appropriately. You can't just see the beauty and grab it. You also need to walk through the garden of your life and be careful not to collect the thorns instead of flowers. Many a person has grown old with a hand full of thorns and a heart full of pain. Then when they look back at their life, they can't even remember the beauty anymore. Their attitude is sour, and their words are negative and critical. The joy is gone, along with their strength.

I went to my first ladies retreat in Arizona in 1986. I was having so much trouble connecting, and the usual mental floggings happened. I am new and a stranger. I am on the outside looking in. I am sure they don't really care to know me. I'll just hang back and watch. One afternoon, I went for a walk, and in the back of the property was an old well half full of rocks with a broken wooden lid on it.

It attracted me for some reason. The Holy Spirit showed up and gave me a picture of myself down in a well where all I could see was a tiny patch of sky. The sky was my small picture of God. He had me read Ecclesiastes 11 and 12, which speaks of growing old and finding God in your youth before your heart gets hard from the evil in the world. He spoke of my sad memories I collected in my heart being like thorns giving me pain and stones holding me down. He said I needed to let him show me a better perspective of my memories. He said I was not feeling connected to those women because of my own feelings of unworthiness that my sad memories tied me to. He said many of the women around me had the same issues. If I wanted out of the well, I needed to start being friendly and talk to the women around me. I found that as I did, I could feel the rocks lifting out of my heart. I would rise higher in the well, and my piece of the sky would get bigger and bigger. When I would hold back, a sad thought would come again, and I would take a rock back and sink a little lower.

What a wise Daddy we have. It is wisdom to look at your life with the end in mind if you ever want to get there with good memories to keep you company. During the following year or so, God would come to me, healing my memories as I would let Him. A few years later in a worship service, in another vision, I could see I was near the top of the well, and I could see a mountain. I was excited to have scenery. That day, I knew I had a hope and a future and it was going to be good. One of my favorite songs says I lift my eyes up unto the mountain from which my help comes. It is God's mountain. Needless to say, I keep talking to women and making friends. My perspective of God has grown sharing life together with them. Nowadays, my only visits to such a well are to help others out of their own. I am pretty sure my calling is helping women with the issues of their hearts.

The wisdom of God always shows up when you need it, whether you are walking with Him in the complex things of life or the simple things. When you have your smartphone on, you have a wisdom app at your disposal—the word (James 1:5). He gives it freely to those who ask.

I remember when my youngest was small, he would stand at my leg and whine from time to time. If I would stop and give him some attention, he would be fine and go on his way. One day, the thought came that I should explain to him he doesn't need to whine. When he felt like that, he just needed to say love and I would stop and give him some. Much to my surprise, he got it. A few weeks later, we were in the waiting room of the doctor's office. Many of the children were whining and tugging on their moms. My son looked up at me and said, "Love." I give him the usual attention and hug, then he went back to his toy. Somehow we got the attention of everyone in the room. "What just happened?" the lady next to me demanded. I meekly explained my process. I got the feeling a whole new world opened to someone. For me it was. I answered my phone when wisdom called.

Call God. He is waiting for you to dial "love." Skip the fussing and turn quickly to Him anywhere, anytime, in any circumstance, and He will always be there to comfort and guide.

One of my points in this chapter is that I have discovered little real wisdom exists outside of that which has been revealed to me by God. Much of man's wisdom has had many failures and turns out to be just vanity at best. *Merriam-Webster* says vanity means "Empty of any real value." The wisdom that really works is no doubt God-inspired, even if man doesn't credit Him with it. Sometimes I hear the wisdom coming out of someone's mouth, but the Spirit of God in me witnesses to me that it is godly wisdom.

I had little understanding of life until I met God. When the Holy Spirit came to live in me, He brought a key to open the door to the wisdom of God. The wisdom of Papa God is an eternal wisdom based on a high love value system. I have found God values life and He values love and relationship so much more than anything else. He values me, and because of that, I can value others. I can only give what I have. His power seems to flow in connection with relationships based in His love.

I have had to let God create a value system in me based on what He deems as valuable, not what sparkles and catches my eye or spurs a whim. I can lead myself astray so quickly. There are times I have caught myself, like a dog catching a glimpse of a squirrel. Gone again!

People are usually in a hurry to get their answers. Most kids are in a hurry to grow up. In my efforts to help them understand how special it is to be a child, I joke around and tell them when you make things, you have to wait for the glue to dry, then for the paint to cure, or else it will fall apart and make a mess. Be patient with yourself.

I love Ecclesiastes 3:

> To everything *there is* a season,
> A time for every purpose under heaven:
>
> A time to be born,
>   And a time to die;
> A time to plant,
>   And a time to pluck *what is* planted;
> A time to kill,
>   And a time to heal;
> A time to break down,
>   And a time to build up;
> A time to weep,
>   And a time to laugh;
> A time to mourn,
>   And a time to dance;
> A time to cast away stones,
>   And a time to gather stones;
> A time to embrace,
>   And a time to refrain from embracing;
> A time to keep,
>   And a time to throw away;
> A time to tear,
>   And a time to sew;
> A time to keep silence,
>   And a time to speak;
> A time to love,
>   And a time to hate;
> A time of war,
>   And a time of peace.

God is the timekeeper. He did not invent the clock. Man invented the clock to control life. I find consulting with Papa God about what time it is, is wisdom. I have also found there is always enough time to do what is mine to do. If there is not enough time, then I

101

am doing things that are not mine to do. Or perhaps I am dragging my feet.

I have found the times of soaking in the presence of God to be like a tuning device. If you haven't discovered soaking yet, it is awesome. Find some time in your busy life to turn on some worship music, lie back, and wait on God's presence.

The hard part is clearing your mind of the many concerns you have. I sometimes have to address them one by one and tell them God has an answer, so go get on the shelf. It helps me sometimes to write them on a piece of paper before I start and put the paper on a shelf. By the time my session is over, I have some of my answers, or at least a better perspective of them. I can now see how much bigger my God is than the problems.

I once tried to learn to play guitar. I love music, but making it apparently is not my gift. I tried to tune the guitar, but I really had no idea what the strings were supposed to sound like. My husband bought me a battery operated tuning device. I loved it when the meter read in the correct zone for a string, indicating it was the right sound. I had no ear for that. I ended up selling my guitar; it just wasn't working for me. I would rather make one than play one.

It is prudent to get in sync with God's timing. I find people who do spend the time soaking go out in the world and become like tuning devices for the rest of the people they are around. When I am losing it, these people help me get back in sync. Sometimes I help them. Stay tuned, my friend.

There are many aspects of wisdom God would like to teach us. A hard one for me was my priorities in life; after

God, family relations come first, not projects. I was forever carried away by the thought I had to earn more money or do more housework or work longer hours.

I know I will get to the end of my life and not wish I had worked more jobs or done more housework. I will want to go back and connect more with my children and make sure they had more of me. It is painful to see the areas of their life where I am sure if I had given more of the necessary good (nurturing) to them, they would not be having some of their struggles now. I have to pray and trust that God can restore for them like He has for me. Today is the first day of the rest of eternity that God has for us.

"Wisdom has a prophetic backbone.

Wisdom is able to see beyond the obvious and discover solutions."

Bill Johnson, June 2013

HE𝒜LING 𝒜N𝒟 WHOLENESS

I learned something today in my devotional time.

I was asking God, "When does the complete manifestation of my healing happen?" The following scenario went through my mind. A couple of thousand years ago, Jesus's back was stripped with a whip, and then He was nailed to a cross. On that day, the gift of my healing was paid for, along with my sin. As with any other gift, there is a day the gift is purchased. There are also the days of preparation for the presentation. Then there is the day when the gift is given. There can also be another day when the gift is actually used.

By His stripes, we were healed means it was a gift purchased a long time ago. The gift was wrapped in Jesus (1 Peter 2:24). The present was given the day you decided you would accept it. It is engaged when you are—it's relational. The gift is really a power tool that comes with an instructor, the Holy Spirit. Training begins in love, truth, and grace.

Some gifts can be given and engaged in a moment's time. If you bought my lunch, that would be a quick gift. When James, my firstborn, was ten years old, he broke his wrist. We had no health insurance because Steve was new at his job. We only had one car that Steve drove to work. We were also new to the area, and had no family or friends nearby. I put my hands on his wrist and said, "God, I need you now to heal my son's wrist." It was quick, so quick, he excitedly ran back out to play. I had to get him to take a breath and appreciate the moment. It was amazing to watch it move back in place.

Other gifts have time lapses. My precious son and daughter-in-law bought me a hand press vegetable slicer in December and gave it to me for my birthday in January. It was my intention to take it with me camping in the summer. I didn't use it at home because I have a Cuisinart. Sadly, on camping day, it got left behind. It is December again as I write this, and I plan to engage my present this summer when we go camping again. Now, if someone gave you a fruit basket, it takes time to eat the fruit and sense the benefit from it. Last year, we gave my granddaughter, Katie, paints, canvas, and brushes. This year, she gave us all paintings for Christmas. The gift of an open door is awesome, but it takes time to see the benefit, and the recipient must engage in the process.

My point here is your gift of healing and other signs and wonders that follow your life were paid for a few thousand years ago. You and the world around you are being prepared to receive your gifts, including healing and other things promised in His word. Sometimes it's instantaneous, and sometimes you have a gift of process. Someone once wrote a song that the ultimate healing was going to heaven. Obviously, getting it in heaven means you didn't get it on earth. The good news is if you accepted the gift of eternal life, which is a relationship with the eternal God, you still have a long time to enjoy your gift.

106

The instantaneous ones are very fun, and you want to jump up and down, rejoice, and give thanks. The other gifts require believing God is who He says He is. The process of testing your faith is wondrous. You are being transformed into the image of your Father in heaven. Like every child, working and playing with dad brings an understanding of who He is, what His nature is like, and how He does things. God created you and me as one of a kind, and He customizes His love relationship with us. The number one prayer always being answered first from heaven is Jesus's request in His prayer in John 17. "Father, make them one even as we are one." It takes a lot of experiences to change your thinking to understand where Papa God is coming from in His process. Patience is a must, believing all the while He is a good God with only our best at heart.

My own thinking can often cause me distress and manifest in physical pain. I hate to think I cause my own grief and pain, but it does happen. For example, if I have started to worry, fret, and get wrapped up in anxiety over the current happenings in my life, I have been known to develop intestinal issues. It takes me a while sometimes to realize it is my own attitudes that can trip me up. Sometimes, I have taken on more than I can handle. Sometimes, life is more than you can handle. I am so grateful that I can go to Papa God, and He is there to take a moment to love me, talk about it, and impart wisdom. He helps me find new perspectives. Trusting anyone, even the wonderful God we have, can be a difficult hurdle. I have not had many trusted confidants in my life. What about you? Seems everyone has a hidden agenda, and sometimes the agenda is even hidden from them.

It has come to me that there is one other point about walking through the trials of life to keep in mind. I often asked Christians I thought were wiser than me for advice in my situations. Many Christians attempted to encourage me with the words, "God will not give you more than you can handle." The truth I found is He often allows the world to pile on more than you can handle, because He doesn't want you to handle it alone. You were not created to be alone. The reality is He will not allow more to come on you than He can carry you through to victory.

I have had ailments I had tried everything for and nothing helped, and then I found something that worked. I thanked God for that something that worked. I have had God heal my child of a broken wrist, yet I have also had two broken wrists of my own. I had to endure two casts and a strange lifestyle for a few weeks. Also, I had to accept help from so many people.

Think about the many things you would need help doing if both of your wrists were in casts halfway down your fingers and up to your elbows. When your fingers more, more pain is created on top of the pain you were already in. Yes, my husband helped me with that, too! (Think about that for a while.) Sometimes, the healing process can be the way you or someone else learn something. I learned more people cared about me than I thought. My husband learned a lot more about what nurture meant.

He didn't cause your issue, make no mistake about that. The sin nature, sickness, disease, and trouble started back in the garden. Never forget there is an enemy to your soul who tries to steal, kill, and destroy you. Your God is exactly the opposite. He is always ready to minister love, life, and wholeness. In evangelistic meetings, many people come away healed. Many won't be healed. I have learned it is God's business. Papa knows best. Just know He always wants you to be healed. He already paid the bill, remember! Sometimes not being healed at the moment has to do with needing a different healing first. You may need a healing that shuts off the running faucet of your current problem. It is like a cold; you have lots of symptoms that are not the real cause of your sickness, that is a little virus you picked up that you can't even see. You may be sick in soul. He has healing for that too.

I have found most of us don't realize how sick in soul we are. Where the brokenness in us happened, we can become sick. That broken place is like a running faucet that needs to be turned off instead of endlessly mopping up after it. We have to ask the Holy Spirit to show us what is broken and what the process of healing is. Mostly, when we follow through on it, God is faithful to heal.

What I may need is to invite Jesus into the moments of emotional injury. How awesome it was for me to put Him in those memories, get His perspective, and let Him heal it. I can forgive all things and move on. Amazing new life comes in when you let the old dead stuff go out. The wounding you received starting in childhood has to be acknowledged, then you can let Jesus and His truths change how you define it. If you don't you end up living out of your wounds, you will miss so much of what God has planned for you. Not to mention the baggage of misery you will be dragging along with you.

A word of caution: Don't just relive your moment over and over, because it will just make a bigger wound. If you ever continually rub on a stretch of healthy skin, you will make a sore. Only go to the memory when you are truly ready to let the Holy Spirit in to heal it. You should always have a spiritually mature and experienced person around to help you. When you are healed, you will be able to testify to your story without the pain, and it will encourage you and someone else.

If healing doesn't come, you need to take special care that you don't become offended at God. Bill Johnson has a wonderful teaching on not getting offended by your disappointments. He tells a story about his own son, who is deaf and been prayed for many times, and is still deaf. They are still believing for his healing and trusting in God's timing. The good part is his son prays for deaf people, and they do get healed. You have to ask yourself would that be happening if he were offended with God.

Being sick in soul often begins in our childhood. I think everyone should take a closer look at the traits of the family they come from so they can set their sights a little more realistically in relationships. You really do marry the family, no matter how far behind you leave them. We were really clueless to this wisdom in the beginning of our old and new life.

My husband and I both brought some trouble, habits, and family traits to the marriage. I'm not telling you that to say you shouldn't marry the person God gives into your heart. I am just saying you might need counseling to overcome some of the issues you will face before they get to be giant obstacles to overcome in your relationship. An ounce of prevention is worth a pound of cure kind of thing. You need someone versed in God's ways and filled with the spirit and heart of God. I have not met anyone who could figure this out and be somewhat prepared without some guidance from wiser counsel. This guidance will best serve you earlier in the relationship than later. The sooner, the better.

We had so many family snarls, as I call them, on both sides. I really don't know how we have made it this far except through acts of God in our hearts and minds. I have had to be committed to letting God transform me with His love relationship and His word. Rules without relationship breed rebellion. Relationship with guidelines breeds peace, wisdom, and cooperation.

One day, I got a call from my mom saying my dad was very ill and they didn't know how long he might live. Steve and I talked it over, and we decided it had been very enlightening to spend time with his dad in Florida; perhaps we should try to mend the fences with my parents in New York. I was really looking forward to spending time with my parents after all those years. However, we were greeted at the bus station by a hostile mother. I knew I would have my difficulties being around her, and did not want my kids to share the experience I had with her growing up. Her hostility was not what I expected at hello. She was in a very defensive mode. She didn't smile, hug, or say hello. The first words out of her mouth were, "Don't expect me to take care of all your brats." This was a thought that never crossed my mind. We did not start off on a good foot, and it didn't get any better.

Apparently, some friend at work was having an issue with being stuck with grandkids more often than she liked. I think this woman complained at great length, and my mother decided that was what I was going to do to her.

A few weeks later, I was excited to find out I was pregnant with my son Steve II. I thought my parents would be happy too. They were not. They were very upset with me that I would want another resource-sucking being. I should want more and better stuff. We all have a grid we view life through. I try to let the Holy Spirit show me when I am looking through a yucky clot in my grid, and then clean it up. My parents bought their grids for understanding life hook, line, and sinker. They were not about to let any other truth in. We spent the year in what felt like being trapped in a soap opera tragedy from hell. I realized why God led me out of the state, not just out of my family life. There was no way they would have ever let growth or a healthy change happen. They clung to their deceptive lies. It was like I was in a snake pit where the snakes were getting bigger and bigger, and one day, they would swallow me whole.

We packed up at the end of a year and moved back to California. That's as far as we could go without falling into the ocean. God graciously provided Steve a career as food and beverage director of a huge downtown hotel in San Jose. We were happy to be free to pursue who God was calling us to be.

Before I accepted Jesus, I saw miracles and was healed. I know better than anyone that those demonstrations of His power don't necessarily turn your thinking or life around. It is His kindness that leads us to repentance (Romans 2:4). Repentance is doing a 180-degree turn in your thinking about God and His way of doing things.

Before I knew God, I once suffered from a strep infection internally. I was treated with all kinds of medicines and was in grueling pain from this flesh eater. If you ever had strep throat, you have a clue. I was lying on my bed in pain, and I asked the God I didn't pray to, "Please let me die today and have this be over." I told him that anyone could be a better mother to my children and no one would really miss me. Much to my surprise, I got an answer. OUT LOUD.

"NO, I have more for you yet in your life." I was healed in that moment. Shocking, yes. I didn't get it yet about Him trying to woo me. Did I immediately turn to Him with gratitude? NO. I had not yet come to the end of myself. In fact, I remember being frustrated and yelling back, "What is it with you, why are you bothering with me?" God knew that in the next year, I would finally remember all the many kindnesses He did for me and open up to let Him in. It is amazing to me that in His love for me, even while I was still filthy with my sin and rebellion, He would heal me.

In 1979, we were in New York. I was pregnant with my last child, and we were living in a third-floor apartment. The old furnace had started slowly leaking carbon monoxide. I spent the most time there, so I was the first to start getting ill. I hurt my hands hanging curtains, and the cuts were not healing. My hair started falling out. Then the kids started to get headaches like the ones I got. We had a visit from a neighbor. A group of interesting people from a church called The Way. They figured out that we were suffering from carbon monoxide poisoning. We quickly found a newer place and moved. I went to my baby doctor, finally. We had no insurance again because my husband had another new job. The doctor was not very encouraging. This was 1979, and he very much believed my baby would be deformed. He recommended an abortion. The year before, God had spoke to me and said I would have a blue-eyed boy. I always attempt to take God at his word. Time wore on, and I began to wear down a bit, listening to the doctor say things like, "Your baby could have a hand growing out the top of his head.

113

You don't want him to live like that, do you?" I prayed a lot, declared God true and every man a liar.

I decided I needed help in this matter. So a couple of weeks before he was born, I went forward for prayer on a Sunday. Great praying, but I had a sense God had not done what He was going to do yet. The next Sunday, I went forward again and talked to the pastor. I told him everything, even about how nice last week's prayer was. But, sir, I need a miracle now.

He called the whole church forward to pray that Sunday morning, and the presence of God came heavy on us; the heat was intense. I could feel the hand of God go straight through me and remake him, like molding clay inside me. I knew my God was there for me. (That smartphone was working.) I opened my eyes and the pastor's eyes were bugging out, they were so wide open. I said, "God is doing it." He said, "I know." We were both sweating from the heat this miracle generated in the midst of us. It is strange to think of how it felt; at that moment, God's hand was like a hot knife passing through butter. The movement inside me was bizarre and exciting.

I know that has not happened for everyone. I can only testify to what I have experienced at the hand of God. I am confident that whatever happens in my life, it is better with Papa God in it than without. Oh, yeah, he was born a beautiful ten-pound boy with blue eyes that stayed blue, and his daughter's and son's eyes are blue too!

God loved us when we were unlovable. Someday, you will figure out all the massive directing of traffic God had to do to get you to this point in your life. You will be blown away.

I live a real life with real problems, like everyone else. A few years back, I was in a series of traffic accidents. In most of them, I was stopped at a stop sign when someone rear ended me while they were talking on their cell phones. I went through lots of complaining to God, "You are supposed to make sure I don't get hurt like that." I have required two back surgeries. Rotator cuff surgery was worse than having a baby. I have had traumatic arthritis in both thumbs from holding the steering wheel, when hit from behind. I actually said, "God, if there is a next one, please let me die in it; this pain is way too much." Through it all, I had a very real sense of not being alone. If you have ever been through painful storms in life, the knowing and feeling you are not alone in it is a huge comfort. I used to be afraid of pain. That fear has definitely disappeared. I started telling people, "Pain is nothing, I eat it for breakfast." I finally can stop saying I would rather die than go through pain. This one fact might be a relief to God. These days, I get up in the morning, declare I feel fine, and God and I will have a great time. I choose to live by God's truth about me, not some feeling the enemy fostered.

I met a lot of nice people while going through all this. The only testimony I could offer was my God was sufficient for me and to keep smiling. God was my strength to quit pain pills and keep going to painful therapy. God has more for me, yet keeps me doing my home exercises. I want to be able to keep up with all He has for me and my grandchildren. Experiencing His love and closeness was amazing. No one wants this kind of experience with pain to find out about this tender part of God, but it is awesome to know it is there for you. I may need that again at the end of my days on the planet. I can take a lot of comfort in knowing it is there for me whenever I reach for it. And I reach for it more and more.

What is up with my body now? I went to every healing line. Something would get a little better. Sometimes it would come back. One day, Mario Murillo was coming to our church. As I was getting ready to attend, I was praying, "God, I have been in too many healing lines, I don't know when or how you will manifest my total healing. God, I am not going to get in another line unless you cue me up. I know I am a little dense sometimes, but you love me and you'll work with it."

I went. Mario is always exciting to listen to, and I was thrilled that so many people were getting words. The presence of God was amazing. I hoped for what I thought was beyond hope for myself, but didn't really expect anything. The service was just about over when he said, "You stand up." I looked around in disbelief, really. It was me! I think if someone points at you and says stand up, it's a cue. Wow! He read my long laundry list of ailments to me, every one of them. He even said the enemy has tried to kill you three times. Then he said, "God says healing head to toe."

Don't know why God does what He does like He does, I am just going to be thankful. In heaven we will get so many answers we don't get here on earth. Some things healed right away. The thumbs are way better. Some things are slower at progressing. I keep thinking there must be a faucet I haven't let God turn off yet. I am thankful we are going in the right direction. Some days a pain will pop up, and I declare, "God said healing and wholeness head to toe; you have no right to be here." Much to my surprise, most times it dissipates. I think I

116

am learning to declare God to be true and pain to be a liar.

In this process, I had to forgive the people who hit my car. I even had to tell God I forgave Him. One of our childlike qualities is that we get mad at our parents for not being what we want them to be for us. Actually, we have that problem with everyone. Forgiving God for letting you experience real life can be huge.

Recently, God brought me back to forgiving Him again. I tried to explain this to some friends. They told me it was not God because it was not scriptural. I had no words from the Bible to support my claim. I went back to God because I know His number. It is on my spiritual speed dial. His response was, "I speak Bible, brain, and heart. Would you not ask your child to forgive you if the pain of what happens exceeds his understanding of the good intended?"

I went to an open table conference shortly after that. I asked Baxter Kruger(Theologen and speaker, wrote the The Shack Revisited) his thoughts on the matter. It actually excited him. He said, "If God said that to me, I would know it was an invitation to talk about something I had not felt safe to put on the table until now. Sometimes, people get confused about the Bible. As wonderful as the living word is, it is not a cookbook." We asked God to show me what it was. God brought me back to myself as a little girl about four, understanding that Mom was not a safe place. I went to my closet, took my favorite dress, and ran away to Grandma's—next door. Grandma sent me back home. On the way home, I cursed myself. I decided there was no one on my side. There was no one to defend me or save me. I was alone and must endure until I could care for myself. The nwxt day I went back to

117

Baxter andwe went through the pain that has happened since, like snapshots, and collected them in an album. Baxter said to ask Jesus to take it away, but He would not. I had to give it to Him. Then I saw Jesus hug my book of pain and suffering until it disappeared into Him. He took it in. It was a treasure to him. It was precious and it was not for nothing. God's app for that.

I finally realized what He meant by "I speak Bible, brain, and heart." In my zeal to heal, I studied the psychology of behaviors. I had been obedient to God in asking forgiveness and writing letters to people. I memorized scriptures from the Bible to speak to the pain when it came up. I had covered the brain and Bible part of healing. The problem was I never let myself totally feel the emotional impact of my losses until I could empty the cup of bitter I had buried where not even I could reach it on my own. I am now finally able to experience a fuller cup of blessing God has for me in all my relationships.

I realize that God is concerned with all the parts of me, like any good parent. I'm learning there are times when the condition of my soul is more important to God than my body. We tend to want the body first because we are prone to pamper ourselves and pad comfort levels. God knows how motivating our discomfort can be. His aim is wholeness from the inside out. Like I have said, sometimes to heal your body first would be like trying to mop up that running water faucet. The smart move is to shut the water off first.

I did not know that I was co-dependent and carried around a victim mentality until God brought me that truth in a dream. Once I received the truth, I had to stick my grappling hook in it and begin my struggle to freedom, healing, and wholeness. (Or was that God sticking a hook of truth in me to pull me along?) I was knocked down so many times, I didn't want to fight anymore. I would enable all the aggressive people around me to have peace. I so didn't want to fight that I let everyone get their way and let go of everything that was me until I felt like I disappeared. This was my true brokenness that God needed to heal in me. He didn't create me to be a non-person. Before I knew Him and when I was newly saved, He did some obvious things to get my attention and encourage me along. As I have grown in relationship, He expects me to do more processing so I will grow stronger.

I remember teaching my kids to play games. I would let them win a lot so they would keep playing and learn the game. Every now and then, I would go ahead and win so they could get a taste of reality and grow some character. As they got older, I would win more and more, until the day they could really beat me. Healing isn't a game to God, but there is an encouragement principle in there that I think He uses in wooing us along in relationship and letting us mature. He is such a good Dad.

There are so many mindsets we humans have developed that don't serve us well at all. I thought giving people what they wanted was making peace. All I made were spoiled, demanding monsters who give you anything but peace in the end.

One of the books I have read that can help you to zero in on the issues that keep you from enjoying the fullness of your life and love relationship with God and others is *Changes that Heal* by Dr. Henry Cloud. He and Dr. John Townsend also wrote the book about boundaries. Besides the Bible, they are excellent places to start your journey to wholeness. These books can give you helpful information that I would stumble through if I tried to give you a meaningful condensed version. I put a small book list at the end of this book. They will be some of the books I have read. It is a small list because I am not that big a reader. I am more of your trial and error kind of person. Audio books are my friends in the car.

The help and healing you need depends on the degree of woundedness you have received from the world and how many lies have been propagated in you. Believing the truth of God will make you free (John 8:32). The problem is finding the real unadulterated truth. We live in a world where, since Adam and Eve met the snake in the garden, someone has had an agenda against the truth to manipulate things to their way of thinking and benefit.

God is the only one who has been thinking of you the whole time. His thoughts for you are as many as the grains of sand on the beach. Yes, that is in the Bible. Psalm 139:17–18. The whole psalm is very moving for me. It even says God has a book all about each one of us. How many of us actually kept up with the baby book about our children? At this point in my life, I wish I had. I had to get old to realize every life is so important to Papa, and a record of what He does in your life is a good thing to have. It can be a gratitude book to help you through the tough times.

I sometimes keep a journal these days. It really helps to process life. I recently heard Julia Child said she wished she'd kept a journal. At least we have her cookbooks.

HOW TO DO IT

This may seem like a funny title for a chapter, but it is very practical. I can't even count how many times things are before me that must be done and I don't know how.

I have asked the Holy Spirit for direction, and He always comes through. I am not the only one to experience this interaction with God. I first learned about this from the man who brought me to the Lord. Hopefully, you read my testimony in an earlier chapter and got that story. When Manual came to fix things in my house he first took apart my toilet. I asked him if he knew what he was doing. He asaid "No, but if God can teach Noah who was a farmer to build a boat he can teach me to do this. Next it was the shower, then the heater. What I thought was mission impossible was the gas stove. Manuel lined all the parts up and down the kitchen in order as he took them off. Every fix I would ask him if he knew what he was doing and everytime he would answer "No, but if god can teach Noah who was a farmer to build a boatHe can teach me."

The story has stayed with me and inspired many fix-it projects and the writing of this book.

If God can teach Noah, who was a farmer, to build a boat, He can teach Dee who flunked Latin, Spanish, French, and English in high school to write a book. Are you laughing out loud with me? He can instruct you too.

When you start reading your Bible stories, you will find many stories like this. God had to teach Adam to be a farmer. He needed to teach Noah to build a boat. He taught David to kill lions, bears, and giants. In the Bible, you will read about who begat who and God giving them skill gifts. These crafts and skills had to be taught by the Spirit of God to those individuals. There were no books on the subjects and no schools for it back then. No one had the skill to teach it. The first time every skill was done by someone, it was taught by the Spirit of God. I wish I could just get zapped by God and know it all in an instant, but mostly, I have to do the process. He needed to teach Moses how to lead Israel as a people. So God had him raised in the house of the king so he would learn leadership skills and have a leadership presence. Then God had him tent sheep for forty years to teach him humility. You need both to lead well. He had to give Moses the book of laws. Now there was a tough book to write.

My first personal experience with this was a couple of years after my adventure with Manuel fixing things in my house. I wanted to cover an ugly chair with some fabric that was given to me. I had no pattern and no clue how to do it. I sat in the chair and said, "God, I need to figure this out, can you help me like you helped Noah and Manuel?" I got up and looked at the chair, and immediately, I started getting these pictures and instructions in my head. Measure this, measure that, and cut the pattern pieces out of newspaper using the measurements you just took. It was very cool. I then got the instruction to sew which pieces together. When I was done, the cover slipped on like a glove. The best part is when a friend visited and looked at the chair, she was amazed at me. She said she never saw a chair cover fit so well. I knew at that moment I had tapped into something. You need to know I was a self-taught sewer, too. I realized in that moment I had been hearing the Holy Spirit and never knew what it was. I got really brave then and sewed up a storm of clothes for the kids and some tops for myself. Recently, one of my girls asked me to sew an article of clothing for her. It looked very difficult, and I think it showed on my face. My daughter said, "Hey, Mom, just work your magic." A piece of me wanted that credit, but I knew better. I have no magic. I do have a heavenly smartphone app and a friend called Holy Spirit. We are on the phone a lot.

Once I experienced success in one area, I started experimenting with food. The kids would tease, "I wonder what's for dinner tonight?" I did not become a gourmet cook, I just learned to cook well for my family. I do make a mean apple pie, if I say so myself.

I put the prophetic chapter before this one because you really do need to train yourself to hear God. It is so important to recognize His way in you. I have found that He is just as thrilled and pleased by these transactions as we are, maybe more. I just read Baxter Kruger's book *The Great Dance*. He talks about everything that is and everything we do all being a part of the community of the Trinity. Every task, every occupation can be an expression of the Glory of God in us. You can feel good about your job, whatever it is. Love, love, love that!

His love demonstrations and communications are peculiar to your relationship with Him. It is very personal and a custom fit. I know I am redundant, but some things bear repeating.

We must be willing to learn like little children. Learn something new every now and then to stay in tune with the process. The process of learning starts out awkward. You're stepping out in the unknown. You have no real concept of what you're doing. You feel inept and insecure, not at all sure of the outcome. We all would rather be confident of success before we do something. That is not the learning process. Thomas Edison had hundreds of failures first. Michael Jordan, who has made the most points in basketball, also made the most misses. Keep experiencing the process; it helps you be humble and builds your capacity for compassion when you are helping others. It keeps you childlike before your Papa and always in need of Him.

I have had many occasions to need to fix my own appliances. It completely amazed me when it worked. I put a sprinkler system in one house we lived in. I prayed, mapped it out, measured for pipes, and counted each kind of joint needed. It turned out awesome. These days, I am very happy to call an appliance repairman and not have to fix so many things myself.

I have made my girls their prom dresses. I made several bridesmaid dresses. I got a phone call from a seamstress who was getting paid to make the same bridesmaid dress I was making. She could not figure out how to put it together. What a moment for me to go and show her how it worked, not because I was so smart, but because I let the Holy Spirit instruct me on how to do it. She was a

Christian, so she was delighted with the whole process. I made a new friend, too.

Our children's ministry had a theme for last summer about being royalty, the whole armor of God and fighting the good fight. They asked for help to create staging for their teaching. Those weeks were so much fun for me and not stressful, even though they asked for things I had no idea at the time how to do. I have created banners and swords with Holy Spirit instructions. The hardest thing was the puppet stage curtains. We have very little storage space. Because we meet in a school, everything has to disassemble and store flat and small. God is so good and faithful. We used threefold display boards for each room and painted them to look like castle walls. I put Velcro on the inside of the curtains so they could come out and everything would fold flat in a bin.

This ability to call God and tap into Him works in every area of your life. When I tried my hand at collage in my fifties, I took an algebra class. I would get stuck so many times trying to figure that stuff out. One time, I went to a math lab, and I was particularly perplexed about the week's problems. I thought to myself, *I can't do this, I need to quit*. I then had the thought, *You have the mind of Christ*. Oh, yeah, I can be smarter than this. I spent a few minutes praying and declaring the truth to myself that I can do this. Quickly, understanding began to come to me. When I was done, I had to go to my car and cry with joy. How faithful and trustworthy is my God!

When God asked me to open a women's recovery center, I had no clue how that would work out. It was a long process. I found God faithful at every step. I needed to volunteer at a place for a year to even find out how it works. Then I had to fundraise. Never did that before. I went with the leader of the ministry to a church for a presentation of their ministry and their appeal for funds. They were gracious enough to let me say a few words about my intentions. They raised a few hundred dollars in the offering. One man walked up to me and gave me a check for $1,000 to start me on my way. God sent a couple of ladies to help. We put on a pastors' free lunch at a hotel to announce our plans and ask for help, and a newspaper carried our story.

Then God said, "Have an auction." That scared the daylights out of me. The first auction was in a warehouse, and we raised $6,000. Then the Lord said, "Plan a dinner auction." I was told about a ministry that matched money you raise. When we raised $40,000, we were matched. We rented a house and opened our doors. I was as shocked as anyone when it really happened.

The how to do it app is for all of your life. The world we live in poses so many situations, and often, we have no idea what to do. God does know what to do. He can see the whole situation from beginning to the end already. The answers you hear may not be what you want, but they are best. There are millions of reasons you don't know yet because you can't see it all from beginning to end. If you could, you would not be learning to operate in faith and trust in God. This kind of relationship with you is the most important treasure to God.

Be kind and patient with yourself. God knows how to cut those giant problems down to size.

POWER

The power struggle of good versus evil in the external world is much more obvious than it is in the internal world. The movies do a great job of displaying that for me. I love superhero movies. The hero has a great powerful might to squash and conquer the bad guys. I want that. Don't you? To me, that would be fun and gratifying; the power to right all wrongs. I believe God could do that. He seems more focused on cultivating our special relationship. He keeps leading me into circumstances that will cause me to call on Him. His strong desire seems to be that I will know Him, grow straight in stature and strong in character to resemble Him. Remember, Jesus prayed the number one prayer over all prayers in the universe. "Father make them one as you and I are one" (John 17:21–22). Then He sent the Holy Spirit to us to fill, help, guide, council, and bring power to live that we would not have otherwise.

I hear people talk about power as the ability to get whatever you want when you want. There is the power to get wealth and the leverage of power to make people do what you want. There is also the power to let a greater good happen.

Jesus had ALL power and used His power to love, free the oppressed, feed the hungry, heal the sick, and show us what our God is really like. He paid taxes with the gold found in a fish's mouth and turned water into wine. Let us not forget raising the dead.

The most important power He had was His life that God gave Him and empowered with a purpose that saved all people. All the people, whether they knew the truth or not. It was about blazing a trail for us to connect with God. (All these stories are found in the New Testament.)

There is a serious connectivity that needs to happen between you and the creative God of the universe. The best story I have ever heard to get this point was told by a pastor I once knew from the Vineyard Church, Blaine Cook. He told the story of his first trip to the ocean as a boy with his family. He was in awe of the ocean, and the waves and stuff that washed up on the shore. He so wanted to posses this wonder. He found a jar with a lid to take a piece of the action home for himself. He piled some sand into his jar, then water, some shells, and kelp. He placed it in the trunk of the car, excited to take the ocean waves home. When he got home, he was so disappointed that the water didn't make waves on the sand, shells, and kelp he had put in there. He waited and watched for days, but all that happened was a really big stink in his room. The lesson learned? A piece of the ocean does not function the same apart from the whole, nor does it stay alive. It is the same with us; we are a piece of God's spiritual ocean, and when we cut ourselves off, we don't operate in the wonder we would have if we were connected. There will be no powerful wave of God. You won't feel the ebb and flow.

128

Eventually, you probably will stink. At least you will develop a lot of stinkin' thinkin'.

When I first discovered my salvation and my God, I wondered why God didn't just fix everything so I could have it easy. I was like many people, thinking I belonged to a special bless me club. That was short-lived thanks to real life in the real world. I so questioned everything, "Why didn't you just make it all perfect to start with?" I had the same childish thoughts we all have. "If you love me, God, you would make my life so easy and give me everything I want." Have you noticed all the kids who grow up that way have a soul full of misery plus emptiness inside that says it is all meaningless and hopeless? They are sorely missing a value system, good character, and a purpose in life. God is a good Dad trying to raise you up with a heavenly value system and the power of loving. I have also seen the kids who grew up with so much trouble, it wounded their souls and crushed their spirits. They were stuck in feeling that things are meaningless and hopeless.

I was hopeless for a while, until I let God love me. My life experience growing up was feeling like the furniture was more valuable than me and being the whipping post for Mom's frustrations in life. I can't begin to tell you how many times I heard her say that her unhappy life was my fault. The veins in her legs were my fault because I was born. She didn't have all the stuff she wanted because she had to spend money on me. More than once when she dropped something, it was my fault because I was there in the room. When I went out on my own, I seemed to attract people to use and abuse me. It is like predators smelling blood from far away. I remember thinking I am so insignificant and do nothing well. If I were to die, no one would notice or care. I was overwhelmed and crushed by my life circumstances. I was carrying the heavy weight of a victim mentality.

When Papa God put His Spirit and love in me, I was not crushed by these things anymore. I am not saying they went away or were not difficult, they just didn't crush me to hopelessness. I knew I had a hope. I knew God knew I was here and cared and would help me find an answer. I was not alone and helpless anymore. Hope is powerful. Like Paul, of the Bible, I can say I have been persecuted but not abandoned, struck down but not destroyed (2 Corinthians 4:9). I am blessed beyond the curse. That is what people who love you do; they walk through it with you. The love and joy you can bring to someone is a powerful healer for the soul. It will heal your soul right along with theirs. It is awesome to watch the snowball effect it has.

The inner battle for good versus evil is not as simple to see sometimes. I remember the overwhelming hopelessness that came when, after much effort, I could not change myself with human efforts alone. I was struggling against all my bad habits and wrong assumptions about myself and my life. That was my stinkin' thinkin'.I have noticed the more I know and understand God, the more power I have over myself and my life, and I am happy about it. It's awesome! I don't have to do some of the things in life I used to think I had to do. I recognize my choices, and there are more of them when I stop and talk it over with Papa God. I don't have to rebel about rules. I can actually choose to want to follow some. That was true power to me. Some of you may not get that, but others of you do. I actually can say no to things these days. I used to feel compelled and enslaved to say yes to everything offered me. I had to do things people said because I could not handle the rejection or consequences that came with no. My mother would get very angry about anything that didn't happen the way she wanted. Those demonstrations really frightened me as a child. I was programmed from childhood to fear other people's anger and to hunger for wanting to be liked and accepted by everyone. At a certain point in my life, getting anyone to like me would do. Now that I like myself, I am free to be me. I might wish you did like me, but I am OK if you don't.

In my full-blown rebellion of that person, as a young adult, I had to act in an in your face manner in the way I dressed and talked. I would do nothing I was asked and was blatant and outrageous. When my personal behavior pendulum swung the other way, I had to be sneaky to do what I wanted. I would be fearful and anxious for everything, and depressed.

I am now free to choose how I talk and dress. I have a new agenda now to express the love God put in me to give you. I want to reflect my Father God in everything. My old agenda was to survive another hour of life with the least amount of pain possible. Avoidance makes your behavior pendulum swing to the extreme with every emotional wind.

I have found my Papa God doesn't deal with me through anger, like my parents, or like the church said of Him. Everything with God is about a relationship of drawing closer and getting to know Him. I enjoy His grace in my life and respect the consequences for my actions. However, His love and acceptance of me is never in question. His corrections always bring joy in the morning.

He already knows me, but apparently He likes to hear me discover who I am and what I think. Hardly ever found anyone who cared what I thought before. WOW! I have learned that this is a basic human communication relationship skill. When you care about someone, if you show genuine interest in where they are at and what they have to say, they will usually care about where you're at and what you have to say. God is good at relationship.

There is influential power in mutually respectful relationships. I have found operating out of respect is one of the major principles of God in us to influence the world to the ways of the kingdom of heaven and the reality of God. There are so many things I wonder why He hasn't fixed. I am guessing it is because He respects me, and you, too much to deny us the freedom of choice and experience of consequence. We learn to sense our own power of choice. Self-control is powerful. In my observations, the people who try to exercise the most power over others usually don't have much over themselves.

You maybe wonder if what you have to say about anything matters much to God. There are many places recorded for us to see that things can be changed by our interaction with God. He is not subject to us; we are subject to Him. He does choose to respond in relationship. I often wonder if those weren't just tests to see if we really believed in the goodness of God. Abraham asked to save Lot and family from the destruction of Sodom and Gomorrah. Moses asked God not to destroy the disobedient people because it would give God a really bad rap on the planet. God did hold back for a while, and by the time the people got to the Promised Land the second time, all the rebellious ones had died off and a new generation stood to inherit the land. These were the children who did not experience slavery or a slave's victim mentality.

I often sense I have walked around a mountain many times until my lack of belief gives way to desperately believing I need to do this. In the New Testament, a woman asked for healing. Jesus replied to her that the bread was for the children. He meant the Jews, the chosen people. She challenged Him that even the dogs get the crumbs under the table. Jesus admired her resolve and granted her desire. These are power moves where I come from.

I don't have power over other people unless they give it to me. We all know about tyrants and bullies who try, and sometimes succeed in, taking power over people. Parents have a power over children, but this power is to oversee their care while they are vulnerable and to see to it they receive the training they need to make a life for themselves. A good parent will transition a child into an empowerd adult.

I am a child of the King. I do have power over the enemy of this life. We do not fight against flesh and blood, but against spiritual wickedness in high places. In 2 Corinthians 10:4, I learned my weapons are mighty to bring down the enemy's strongholds. What is a stronghold? It is a lie or a destructive habit that you have practiced so long it has taken on a life of its own, governing you.

I have wrestled with this problem many times. I have let myself believe the enemy and he made strongholds in my belief system, giving misperceptions and lies a high place above all other truths and beliefs. I found that in my life, I am constantly weeding out these lies and misperceptions from my mental beliefs, as the Holy Spirit brings more and more understanding of the truth that originates from heaven and is always confirmed in the Word.

The lies seem to begin their own form of government in a life. They begin to dictate what I can and cannot do. These dictates have found their way to overriding what God would ask of me. Ever hear yourself say, "I can't, I am not smart enough, I don't have the resources, and I'm nobody." Gotcha!

Adam and Eve fell prey to the enemy casting doubt on God and their relationship to Him. The lie of the enemy caused them to override the truth of trust in His goodness in their relationship to him.

Lies seem to even have their own military defense weapons. Anyone else noticed religions taking on one aspect of the Bible or God and building a fortress around it with endless rules and regulations? Many a church and parent have excommunicated a child for their thinking that doesn't fit in the box they made. That is not my loving God.

We have all taken our turn at arguing our point of view. So often, I have gotten stuck in thinking my way of thinking has to be the right way, after all, I believed it all my life. Maturity has a way of showing you things you don't like to admit about yourself. The sooner I admit it and open up to what God is trying to show me, the sooner I mature and get healed in that area.

Selfishness is one of those things that can be a tyranny like no other to live under.

The power God is giving doesn't flow through the selfish. Once you can see it in yourself, accept the fact it is there and deal with it, because we all have it to some degree. What child do you know who hasn't acted like it's all about ME! Have you ever looked at an adult all twisted up about a small thing that wasn't just right for them and thought, get over it, it's not all about you. I have found this a very common ailment in marriage, on both sides.

I wish I could say it was all him but it is not. Giving the it's all about ME thinking the number one spot in your mind will render you powerless to make a pleasant life.

We can never solely make ourselves truly happy. We are happiest making someone else happy. When I am truthful with myself, I know this, and I know someone else's kindness to me makes me happier than my own self-indulgence. It certainly does last longer.

The power to make someone happy is awesome. My mother was a very unhappy woman. Everything needed to be perfect in order for her to be happy. Life and people are never perfect. I had hoped all my life to make her happy, but it never happened. I could not break the tyranny of the misperceptions that governed her belief system.

In the beginning of my salvation adventure, circumstances in my life were subject to a hidden belief that Jesus overcame everything in the world except for my issue. I was more comfortable with the tyranny of the lies and misperceptions I had than the truth of God I had not experienced yet.

Oswald Chambers talks a lot about Paul the disciple. When you first meet Paul in the Bible, he had a passion for a religious cause. After he had an encounter with the reality of Jesus, it caused a huge paradigm shift in his life. He had a passion for God, the love and truth of God, and he set out to tell everyone the really good news.

In reading about this, I noticed he was not as troubled as I would be by all the things that befell him. He believed these things kept him in unmoved devotion to the God he loved, the one who first loved him. I can imagine him remembering Jesus said that they would have tribulation in this life, but not to despair because Jesus had overcome the world.

The trials of this life with the whispers of the enemy in my ear have caused many doubts to arise. I have found following Jesus's example in declaring the truth about me and my God will chase those doubts and the enemy of the soul away, like the sun chases out the night. There are days I can hear the high noon music of a gunfight in a Clint Eastwood movie. Go ahead, make my day!

Best to remember the devil only has the power we give him when we doubt the truth. Fear is the great power drainer. My God has great power, and He has said He resides in me. Just because it is in me doesn't mean He's diminished in power in any way. Power to overcome lies are in the truth. The truth can heal many things in a life. One of my big truths is I am accepted and not rejected.

Jesus was the curse nailed to the cross, so no curse has a reason to land on me. No curse spoken by any man or woman or myself over myself. If, however, I believe this to be truth, it will act as a power until I unseat it with my God-given truth. No curse of the generations of my family, physical, emotional, or spiritual, have any rights to me because of the price Jesus paid. That's power people! Declare it to be true about you. He owns all of it, never again to be addressed by me or anyone else without His permission.

Woohoo!

I pray to be 100 percent one day at being of the same mind as Father God in all matters I have addressed in this book. I have my grappling hook thrown up to the truth I see, and I am staying the course, making the trek. Some days it seems a snap. Some days it seems so hard. I know the journey is better than the alternative.

Here are some words by Philip Brooks I keep posted on my desk:

Never pray for an easier life,

Pray to be a stronger person.

Never pray for tasks to equal your power,

Pray for power to equal your task.

Then doing your work will be no miracle,

You will be the miracle!

I believe we are in the era where the Spirit of God is being poured out on all flesh, as the Bible states. It is the time when the healing line will not just be in churches or meeting tents. The healing lines will be wherever we are standing. I believe God is pulling us into relationship with Him so we, **the nobodies**, will be praying for people and circumstances and will see things happen, to our amazement. We will finally shine as the light of the world, like Jesus. We the children will find the courage and belief to stand and live out our faith, as Jesus did. We are going to get an active revelation of the same spirit that was in Jesus.

That power is alive and well and moving through us. One day, all the signs and wonders following will amaze us. Start practicing your authority, you will amaze yourself.

Ready...Set...

RESCOURCE AND PROVISION

No matter what is going on in your life, God has a plan for your welfare and not your destruction. David in the Old Testament said he had never seen God's own beg for bread (Psalm 37:24–26). Do you consider yourself His?

When I have a need arise and commit it to God, there is no telling on what wings it will come. Isaiah in the Old Testament was sent to a brook in the wilderness during a drought, and the ravens dropped meat from the king's table. I don't think I would like my food carried in by bird beaks or claws. I guess if my other choice was starving, though, I might. Suddenly, the brook dried up and the birds stopped coming. God sent him to a widow who was about to bake her last bread for her son, then lay down and die. God decided it was time to do a miracle and gave her a new business supplying everyone around her with oil. He did that because she complied with the instruction of the prophet. Then God stopped the drought. Go figure. When the children os Isreal were wandering in the desert God droped mana from heaven. In the New Testament, we have Jesus feeding thousands with a few loaves of bread and fishes.

God's promise to take care of you doesn't usually happen the way you expect it to.

Sometimes, it is all about timing. Eventually, we all experience that He waits until the last second, but He is never too late. We live on a finite clock with our little view of things, and God is on an eternal timeline with a bigger picture of your life, and everyone else's along with it. Wisdom reminds me some things we do are like spitting into the wind, a pretty instant return, while others take much longer, like waiting for your hair to grow. Hair growth is only half an inch a month. Growing a baby takes nine months. I hear bamboo takes five years to pop out of the ground. Abraham was one hundred before he fathered Isaac.

In the beginning of our marriage, my husband was in the service, and I was to pack up everything and travel by bus from Hanford, California to Oak Harbor, Washington. I needed to fit our lives in a certain number of boxes that would fit on a bus. We didn't own any luggage at the time. You need to know that I was five months pregnant with twins, and I was huge. I also had a six and a seven-year-old. I was struggling to pack it all up and mind my frisky kids. My friend, Linda, who was to drive me to the bus station was late. When she arrived, she said, "Well, maybe tomorrow." I said, "Oh, no! My husband will be waiting at the bus terminal many miles from the base, and I have no way to call him." She argued that the bus was to leave in five minutes, and it was a half hour away. I said I didn't care. God help me, I have to catch that bus somehow. We loaded her car and I made her take me to the bus station in the next town, called Goshen. I know she did it just to watch me be proved wrong about my new God trip. When we got there, imagine my delight to find out the bus had a flat tire and they were running an hour late. I think this was a one-time grace ticket for a newborn in the kingdom. It is a big stone of remembrance for me. I employed my app of provision, "Papa, I gotta catch that bus." I didn't know how it would work out, I just knew in my innermost parts it would somehow. There just wasn't another answer; God moving was my only hope for the moment. Linda was speechless and bewildered at first, then she said "Your God is as crazy as you are." We piled all the stuff on the bus and hugged good-bye.

When the twins were three, we lived in California, and again, my husband lost his job. We sold most of our furniture to get food and then we ate it. And still no job.

My husband was out looking for a job one day; I think he took an extra long time that day because it is hard to tell your family you can't buy food. This is where someone else's stone of remembrance helped me out. I had heard a missionary in our church talk about an avalanche that trapped some people in a tiny village for a month or so. They were unable to get food or wood. When the supplies ran out, the believers prayed for God's help. It looked like God had not heard them. When rescuers finally arrived, everyone who had been praying was healthy and well. Those who did not were sick and suffering from the cold and malnutrition. I hid that concept in my heart.

Now it was my turn to be out of food. I put a tablecloth on the floor, sat the kids around it, and thanked God for taking care of us. If we didn't get food for dinner, then God, you wanted us to fast and pray. Amen.

Knock on the door.

There at my door stood a weeping woman who said, "Do you need food? You don't know me, but when I passed by your house this morning, God said to buy you groceries. I have fought this all day until I no longer could, so I bought food." She had bought everything from hot dogs to steak to cereal to cookies. She missed nothing. I could not thank her enough. She was amazed she had heard God so clearly. Her heavenly smartphone was on and it rang all day until she answered. I think she shocked herself. We both had a new definition of God and how He moves in us. My husband was really shocked to come home to food. Dinner picnic style on the kitchen floor was even fun.

Praying for a job took much longer. We had an offer from my husband's father to come stay with him in Florida to help us get on our feet. So we commenced the long drive from California to Florida with all we could fit in and on a station wagon, including four kids and two parents.

They lived a much more ordered life than we did. Winter Park inhabitants are a bit more upper-crust than we were. It was a little close living with us there. His dad had married a woman with two boys between the ages of my twins and the two older kids.

We did find a nice church family. I shared with some people how we got there. The God of heaven was full of surprises. Steve got a job, I got a job. We put some money aside to get our own place. One day, I got a call from the church office saying a member of the congregation had a house for rent and were willing to rent to people with four children. That is a miracle! If you have ever tried to rent with more than the standard two kids, you know what I mean. I was very excited. Then I realized we had no furniture. Time to make the call!

"God, I guess we take the first step and you will take care of the rest." A mere twenty minutes later, the church called again and said someone had furniture, and did I want it. Is that spiritual whiplash or what?

We rented a U-Haul and picked it up that very day. You don't want to let someone's decision to give it away sit too long. They could change their minds. We stood in his dad's garage looking in amazement. The furniture was so much better than all we had left behind. There was a living room set and bedroom set. His dad had a table for us, and we found some bunk beds at a garage sale we could afford, as well as some chairs. It was so exciting to watch how God put our life together again.

The lady who gave us the furniture was engaged to be married in New York. She had thought of selling the furniture for money and decided the process was not worth the money that was being offered for her goods. She decided the blessing God would give her would be greater than the cash because she gave it away. She actually left the next day happy as a clam, and so were we.

There have been times where I have scratched my head and just had to be content with believing God knows best. My example for this is when all five kids lived at home and the washing machine went out. I prayed for a washer, because who has money for a laundromat when you are the parents of five kids. Our neighbor across the street just happened to want to get rid of a spare garage refrigerator and gave it to us. I thought how nice, I will put it in the garage for a second to hold all the (never enough) food we have to buy to feed five kids. I made a few trips to a laundromat, groaning at being put out this way. When returning from the last trip, I discovered that our own refrigerator had died. Good thing for us there was a spare in the garage. Ya think?!

That week, my husband received a surprise bonus, just enough to buy a nice little used washer. To me it was always an awesome miracle to have provision for what you need. He knew better than I how soon I would need a refrigerator. That was some kind of app for that.

I don't ever remember being bratty and demanding the best of everything. There is certain contentment in being satisfied with what God provided. I really attributed my status quo to God training me up in the way I should go. I try to be very careful to keep a grateful heart. My groaning at the laundromat showed me who I really was and became a good life lesson for me. The scripture says His eye is on the sparrow and He clothes the lilies of the field. How much more does my God watch over me, His child who chooses to live under His wing? My smartphone is running hot and my stones of remembrance are piling up.

So many times in our life, Steve's jobs have expired and we wondered how we would get by. God would pull out another job like a rabbit out of a hat. All we could do was be in awe of the provision of God.

I came to realize building my faith and the condition of my soul was more important to God than anything else.

We tend to want everything else first because we are prone to pamper our comfort levels. God knows how motivating our discomfort can be. His aim is wholeness from the inside out. There is a scripture where the apostle Paul writes that his prayer is that we should prosper as our soul prospers. Soul prosperity would be the God of all creating His life in you.

Have you read about those people who win the lottery? The ones who were dirt poor and then had so much money, they squandered it all until they were back where they started. How about some of the rich and famous who turn to drinking and drugs, then suicide. Even though they had all they wanted, it did not help them as people with pain-filled souls. Meaning, purpose, and contentment with life that produces inner joy only comes out of the relationship with the Trinity (Father, Jesus, Holy Spirit).

When the twins were in high school, I started working at Meier and Frank, a local department store here in Oregon where we live now. One day, I thought, "God, you said you are the one who signs my paychecks. This year, the company has decided to not give raises. You said you bless your children and rewards are in your hands. I would like a raise, please." An hour later, I was working at my cash register when my daughter called. My grandson Mike was a baby, so she had taken a job as a nanny to be with him and earn some extra money. She had graduated with an early childhood education degree, so it was a perfect fit. The sister of her employer had just had a baby and needed a nanny. She asked if I would consider a job change and become a nanny. It was exactly the raise I was looking for, and I didn't have to work weekends anymore. Thank you, Papa! I loved every minute of being a nanny. I got to utilize everything I had learned in years of experience. It was very redemptive to feel like I was finally doing it somewhat right.

For about three years recently, I was the caregiver for my mother-in-law. I never dreamed that day would come. God blessed her with a job after her divorce, and she earned a good wage and now gets a social security check and a little pension. It would be enough if she could care for herself. At eighty-two, she needs a little help, and the finances she does have are not enough to last very long for the extra watching over she needs. This new task in life allows me to examine myself. Who do I want to be and what shape do I want to be in when I am her age. This begs the question, "What do I need to do to help my body get there better?" Betty White is kind of my hero, at ninety-two and having such a sense of humor and get up and go. I am hoping she will go to at least a hundred before God calls time on her. I am sixty-eight this year, and my health has had its issues. These things could cause me concern. So could the fact we have no retirement fund. This is where I count on my stones of remembrance and punch the app for that. My God has cared for me thus far, and He still loves me. He will step into my future too. Who knows, maybe you all will love my book and I can start a retirement fund. LOL.

I received an invite to accompany a conference speaker to Kenya this year. I needed to raise my own funds. On social security, there is not extra money for these things. Even more impossible were the hurdles of travel, security, my husband's fear for my life, and everyone saying don't go because it is not a big or famous ministry. Pulled out my app for that. "God, if you want me to go, you have many impossible things to overcome." My real lifeline was I knew I heard God say, "Go." I did not argue with anyone. Declared peacefully to everyone God has an answer for your every doubt and question. I kept declaring to everyone, "But God said go." I was totally amazed at how God brought the money together. It was not in really big chunks. He brought it in small amounts from here and there, family friends selling some craft items. The exact amounts needed as I needed. The money for food on the trip came the night before I left, in envelopes on my doorstep. The church in Kenya made sure there were no less than eight people in our five-passenger car for our security, wherever we went. I texted my husband every day to tell him all was well with me. God did amazing things on the trip. The prophetic word before we left was God would bring a new fire to Africa. This was confirmed when we arrived. The Bishop said he had a dream that a white team would come and bring new fire. We were the first white women to come to that area. On the second day, our main speaker was ill, and I was called upon to speak. God was so faithful to bring His words to my mouth. They got to hear many of the testimonies in this book. In this conference, you are on the podium for a very long time. They were excited to receive the message of God's love and that He is a good Father and not out to get them.

Bethel Church worship team sings a song: "He is a good, good Father. That's who He is and He loves me. That's who I am."

FYI, if you were wondering what that drawing is at the beginning of the chapter, it is an ear of corn. I wish I knew why, too! I am sure it is not GMO. LOL.

I did recently hear that an ear of corn is the symbol for abundance in some foreign countries. Perhaps that was God's point.

BIBLE

The dictionary describes the word Bible as a publication that is preeminent and authoritative. Works for me!

For the word that God speaks is alive and full of power; it is sharper than any two-edged sword, penetrating to the dividing line of the breath of life (soul) and [the immortal] spirit, and of joints and marrow.

Hebrews 4:12 (Amplified Bible, Classic Edition)

Lots of my problems have been cured by applying the word in my Bible to my situation.

When Lucifer tempted Jesus to turn stone into bread, He threw the word at him, "Man does not live by bread alone but from every word that proceeds from the mouth of God." The word used there meant in the moment the word is spoken to you, called rhema word.

The Bible is the logos, word of God that he has breathed on. If it has God's breath, then it is living, like Adam after God breathed on Him mud pie man. To me, that makes the Bible the rhema word, too. The word is a tool, a weapon, and wise counsel when you need it.

We were given the Ten Commandments to let us know when we were not in right relationship. This is the great plumb line. If I am not practicing these, I really haven't spent enough time being loved by Papa God. If you find them difficult, I suggest you find someone who understands what Jesus did for you to help you see what's up with that. I am thinking if you read the previous chapters in this book, you may have some idea of what I am talking about.

There are stories in the Bible to help show me how God sees things. There are stories to show me God has diverse and unpredictable ways of handling the issues of life. Everything in my life is custom designed for me and Him to know each other.

I can always see He has a greater thing in mind; well, eventually, anyway. He sees what I really need, not what I think I need. The stories in the Bible and from people have helped me to expect something unique from my Papa to help me in my situations. The Bible says in John 1:12 that to those who believe, he has given the right, and to those who receive Him, the power (the ability) to **become** the children of God. **To become** means we are in a process. Did you notice the difference? You can have a right to something, but receiving it is another step. That step is walking with God.

I have heard New Age people speak of spiritual alchemy. Alchemy itself is a power or a process of changing something common into something precious. The New Age spiritual process is about applying a story to your life, like *The Wizard of Oz*. You then ask yourself, "Where am I in this story?" and you're supposed to be able to see what is next or an outcome. I do not know much about the New Age stuff, but I discovered there is a spiritual aspect to applying the stories in the Bible to my life. These stories are true, and the outcomes are true. The people in the Bible are my witnesses to the fact that God is faithful and has a hand in my life. He has a bigger plan. I can take courage from David and his trials, successes, and failures. He is still remembered as the one called a man after God's own heart. I am after His heart, too. He has the only pure one. The heart of gold to suffer so much for me, then lay down His life. When I face huge obstacles in my life, I can find myself in David's shoes, facing situations seemingly like giants to me. Many things may be at my disposal, like Saul offering his sword and armor. David chose what was tried and true in his relationship with God. He saw the giant coming against the children of Israel as the lion and the bear coming after his sheep. He knew his God was with him to protect his sheep. He knew God was with him to protect His people. I know that my God is with me and has faithfully brought me through every challenge when I have stood up and faced it with Him.

When I make mistakes, I know he is the God of second chance. I read that He forgave the woman at the well and the woman caught in adultery. He forgave Peter and restored him, even after denying him three times. Too bad Judas didn't really know Him, or he would have turned to him instead of suicide. Who can say what happens inside a man to make him not turn to the one who loves him, the one who kept trying to communicate that He came to take away the guilt and the shame he couldn't bear.

I think if you just focused on the wisdom of the book you would be ahead of everyone.

Anxieties are released when I begin thinking about the things God pointed at to think about.

To paraphrase Philippians 4:8, Whatsoever is pure and holy and of good report, honor and the goodness of God

I had so many things released and begin to change in me when I started picking out scripture, proving God to be true, and telling people what God had done for me in light of walking in the truths of the Bible. In the family I grew up in, the practice was just the opposite, and it has taken a lifetime to turn around the lies upon lies I believed. It has been well worth the efforts to get to know God and His truths.

As taught in Revelation 12:11, we overcome by the blood of the lamb (Jesus's sacrifice) and the word of our testimony. That means I am forgiven, all debts are paid, and there are no chains on me. I will testify and speak out about the goodness of the Lord to me.

So much was resolved for me when I could trust He had and still has my best in mind. It often doesn't really look like it. Is that not when faith and trust proves itself? It is not head knowledge; it is only by walking through the experience that it becomes real for you. Many truths can be made known to you in various ways, but you need to prove them out in your life to claim them as your truth. Then you know they are really true.

You do have to know what is says and trust it is true to use it as a tool or a weapon for your life.

I have to tell myself the truth when life looks like it is unraveling and I think I am going down in flames. The truth is God has a plan for my welfare and not my destruction. If I suffer loss, I gain something greater in a greater trust for the one who keeps me. I have experienced a measure of success in my life, and it is not measured in the number or quality of my possessions. It is in the quality of my relationship to Papa God, who loves me, and to those I am privileged to have around me as family and friends.

Romans 8:28 states, "All things work together for good to those who love God." This one helps me keep from despairing over my mistakes. Now they are the new design elements of my life. I learned that phrase from my crafting friends. Our artsy mistakes are new design elements in our projects. Thank you, my Wednesday Gathering ladies group. It is so much better to have a life full of design elements than just mistakes.

This mindset helps me be like God, too. When people come against me, I am learning to turn a situation around. When one of my children learned to count, she figured out that I was pregnant when I married her dad. That just happened to be the year I got saved.

Like a true child, she decided to bring her revelation up at a table full of my new Christian lady friends. I did not get too embarrassed or angry with her. I said, "Yes, sweetheart, that is part of my testimony of God's grace and mercy in my life that I can thank Him for." The seemingly long, dead silence was a little unsettling, but finally, one woman said, "That was so wonderful, the way you handled that. I would have fainted if my child did that to me." I told her God was gracious and kind to me, so I could afford to be that way with her. I gained an open door with those women for many fruitful moments in our time together.

Oh, yes, the child and I did have a little chat about it at an appropriate time, to discuss her revelations. I also challenged her that she knew what she was doing and wanted to see what I would do. It was not a kind intention. We both deserved the kindness of God.

Most of us think at the onset of our walk that there is no time to read that enormous book. Our concept of time can shut the door in the face of wisdom and the work of the Holy Spirit. In this day and age, we are all too busy to take time for some things that are important. With five kids, a husband, and all that goes with that, I thought for too long I could never read the whole Bible. I knew I was terrible at focusing on what I was reading, so I was very attentive to anyone talking about scripture. It soon became apparent to me I needed to know what it said in the book for myself. People smarter than me were fighting over what it said.

I started by putting the Bible on the back of my toilet. Every time I went in the bathroom, I read some of it. I had to pray first because it seemed hard. I soon learned it really was the living Word (Hebrews 4:12). The more of the Word I read, the more I wanted. I suddenly realized there was time to read in my life. I just needed to start doing it and it made its own place. It was interesting to see how my hunger for the Word found time to read it. It was much like wanting food. If you are really hungry, you find some way to get some in you. It created such peace inside me. I could see parallel situations in my life where I had to make choices that the people in the Bible had to make. Of course it looked different, but the crux of the matter was the same.

Usually, it came down to this, will I trust God to be who He said He is, My provider, lover of my soul, my protector, and my ever present help in time of need. The choice was to declare God to be true and all men a liar, or cry and complain about the circumstance, blame others, and be a victim. Will I choose to wimp out and hide in drugs or a bottle or under my covers with a bag of Oreos (or maybe two bags and "got milk!")?

I needed to decide up front that God has a plan for my welfare and not my destruction, and it is a truth I can trust (Jeremiah 29:11).

A life lesson born in experience: you never make the right decision in crises. You need to be armed with the truth and your decision made to stand on that truth before you get to that place. You need your weapons on hand. In the middle of your battle is not the best time to be looking for a weapon.

There is nothing like getting on your face and spending the time to come into agreement with God about your circumstance. Soaking in His awesome presence, however you can get there, is up to you. You will know it is right if you have the Word somewhere in you. The book says that the Holy Spirit will bring His word to your remembrance.

I am hoping you accept the Bible as the true word of God. I have experienced people in controversy over the different versions that have been written. I like the New King James. Let's face it, Jesus was Hebrew, and He didn't talk with thee and thou. No one in the Bible was a proper Englishman. They spoke Greek, Latin, Hebrew, Italian, some Spanish. Most of the texts were all original Greek and Hebrew, I have been told.

The book and religion problem started with organized church. In the beginning of Christianity, you were killed if you were a Christian. Then Constantine was saved, and you were killed if you were not a Christian. Even being saved, as a control freak, Constantine did not have his many controlling mindset issues changed instantly. We don't either. Remember, it is a process to become like His child. It takes time to see and think things the way God does, even after our hearts find this true love.

Constantine ordered all the manuscripts pulled together as a book. He knew with such little organization we humans do what we always do, create our own versions of how it ought to be. Have you noticed some organized religions are still doing that? Constantine wanted only one version—his—so he enlisted scribes of the time to put it all together. They began to fight about what should go in and what should stay out. Constantine finally gave them a deadline, a true dead line: you get it together by this date, or you're dead. What a motivator. I guess that is why he conquered so much of the world then. I am not a Bible scholar or history professor, so if you want more formal verbiage, you're going to have to do your own research. I am just about the short version.

Well the book did get together. Sometime later, good old King James decided it needed to be in the king's English, so he commissioned more scholars and scribes to do that. The New King James is relatively that translation in modern English. Lots of people have tried to write their version of the word. I usually pick the ones that tell me they were directly translated from the original language. I think you get closer to getting what they were trying to communicate. Some of the paraphrased ones are fun to read to help you open up the meanings. I like Peterson's *The Message Bible* the best. The *New Spirit-Filled Life Bible* taught me a lot. I think I gleaned the most from my *Master Study Bible*, with all the history and footnotes they put in. The related history accounts help you get the bigger picture. Knowing the context things were said in helps to interpret it more correctly.

One study that has really stuck with me for whatever reason is the one on the oaks of righteousness. Isaiah 61:3 talks of us as the planting of the Lord, oaks of righteousness. The study at the bottom of the page gave a history of the reference for the term. In biblical times, when they cleared a field for planting, they cut all the trees down. If an oak tree grew back, they would oil it and burn it. If the tree grew back again, they decided the Lord God wanted it there and called it an oak of righteousness. I think it is a cool story. I am guessing I identify with the tree, cut down, burned, but still standing and growing.

I know it is easy to be intimidated by Bible scholars and the people around you who boast of their lengthy Bible reading. Your relationship with God far exceeds the book, but you still really need to read the book. Most of us read the New Testament first because we need to know Jesus. The Old Testament is the history of God creating and dealing with His children, the good, the bad, and the ugly.

Hold your feet to the fire and read even the tiniest part every day. You will surprise yourself. It is living Word, and it will create life in you.

SERVICE

I have heard so many complaints from good souls about getting into connection with the body of believers.

The fastest path to connection, growth, and healing I have found is serving somewhere. It doesn't have to be big or impressive. Actually, the less impressive the job, the more you grow and heal. We are all somewhat pointy in areas of our lives. In working with other people, those points get knocked off. Even if we don't want them to be off, they need to be off. God is smoothing you out to fit together with the rest of the family. It is only when we fit together that we see a truer, more complete picture of who our Papa God is and what He is up to. We also figure out who we really are to Him and to ourselves, and then to the people around us (1 Peter 2:4–5).

I have watched many wait by the wayside and leave it to others to do the chores of the house, for many reasons.

Too busy…everybody is.

I am not worthy…no one is.

I am not called…The gift of help is a call for everyone.

Not Holy…God loves you, you're Holy. Holy only means set apart for God. Jesus made the Holy Family Holy. Get that spirit, and you're Holy, too.

159

No talent…How much talent does it take to fold chairs and stack them or just assist someone? What about to buy cookies to give away or say a kind word. How about smiles!

People don't like me…Really, have you tried these people? People like people who like people.

I don't like people…Tap that love of God the Holy Spirit shed abroad in your heart. Get over and out of yourself. Be more accepting of those differences. GRACE for all.

I don't know anybody…The shyest person can help on a clean-up committee. Those people are so grateful for help, they will consider you a hero.

Some of my most meaningful moments with people and God were late- night clean-up committees. Clean-up committee is my favorite job. No stress to perform. No spotlight. Not so much rushing to get it all done, except the janitor wants to turn out the lights and go home. I found the people on clean-up so friendly and open. Usually, the conversations get to a deeper place, where you share and pray for each other.

It is the best place to break in. I have had the unique fortune of having moved a lot. I am talking from state to state moving. So I am familiar with the problem of connecting. I worked clean-up, sacked lunches for a bus ministry, helped set up chairs and take them down for events. One connection would lead to another. I have made wonderful friends this way. You need friends who go to the deep places with you. Many people's lives don't run in the same circles, but the more we served together, the deeper we have gone.

Other ways to serve can be giving money or other things. It doesn't matter what or how, just find a need and fill it. You will get your socks blessed off. Give food, stuff, your time, sign up for Angel tree, anything, just start giving. Have a generous attitude in all things.

Papa God loves a cheerful giver. Your soul will love you for it, too. There is so much joy to be tapped in giving. Remember, you can't out-give God. The Word says give as unto God and he will repay you tenfold.

A few scriptures to back me up: Proverbs 19:7, Mathew 6:4, Mark 10:21, Luke 6:38, Acts 20:35 and 2 Corinthians 9:6.

Early in my walk with the Lord, I was figuring out there was something unique going to happen with my life. I just didn't really know what at that point. God just kept coming in different ways.

One day while in a worship service, the Lord caught me up in a vision. It was like an overlay reality of the one I was physically in. In the vision, I was standing on a small mountain, and then God brought my mountain to His huge mountain and I knelt before Him. He touched both my shoulders with a sword, like a king knighting a soldier. I laid out both hands, palms up. God took the sword and placed it across my hands. I remember noticing how he labored to put it there as gently as possible. When I looked at my hands, they were bleeding. It was a very sharp two-edged sword. I remember also looking inside myself and crying, because the courage to do what would be required was not in me. I looked up into Jesus's eyes and as I fixed my gaze on Him, I began to be filled up, from my toes to the top of my head, with courage and all else I would need. Then the vision was over. I spent years trying to interpret this vision. From this vantage point in my life, I can see He needed me to get the message that I needed to keep looking to Him for all I needed to live my life and stay the course. I definitely feel like a chosen child.

At one church, I taught two to four-year-olds Sunday school class. This was my training in Bible stories.

I had not read a lot of the Bible yet. Every week, I needed to prepare my lessons. That meant I had to read the story from the Bible. Then I had to understand it enough to communicate the essence of the story to little people.

I would bring props and perform a little one-woman interactive show. When it was Jesus feeding the multitudes, we ate tuna sandwiches I handed out from a basket, followed by cookies, of course. The Good Samaritan was really fun—everybody got bandages and Band-Aids and Popsicle sticks for splints. I did have to explain to parents that their children were not wounded. The reward for me came in the following weeks, talking with parents, making friends, and hearing all about how their little person was praying for their friends and wanting Band-Aids for the scraped knees of their little friends.

The kids actually wanted to say grace and see how many leftovers there were. I loved it.

When my kids started high school, I volunteered to be a support leader in my church's youth group. Little did I know that was as much about me as it was about them. The seriousness of being an ambassador of Christ hit home. You better know your God to run alongside a teenager. Being a teenager for God is getting tougher and tougher. You really need a how to do it app for that.

Teenagers are trying to walk right with so much misinformation in their heads. Add in changing hormones and their ever changing bodies, then the insecurities of discovering who they are and who people and the media say they should be. It is so much harder to get it right these days than when I was a teen. I couldn't even do it then. I made incredible friends in this group, some of them in my age group and some much younger. We went through much growing up together. Some are still connected on Facebook.

The mission trips tested the mettle of us all, and God did his refining work. Leaving your comfort zones makes you vulnerable and able to see much more clearly your need for the guidance of the Holy Spirit you got as an engagement present when you accepted Jesus as Savior and Lord. So if you want to grow, serve somewhere. You will soon figure out that friendship with God is working alongside Him in serving His people.

In Arizona, I volunteered to work with a prison ministry. I had many reservations about doing so. I complained to God that I had spent many years in the faith trying to leave all my street savvy behind. "So you see, God, I won't really be effective here, because they will run their game all over me." Well, God's ways are not man's to figure out.

Here is the God response. I was in the kitchen cooking, and my youngest son was next to me on a stool, as he always had done. In our old house, the kitchen was a lot bigger. He was a bit closer in that townhouse kitchen. He had taken up wearing a nylon vest that scooped down in the back. You have probably seen them. They cover your behind when you sit down so you don't flash your underwear. He turned his back to the gas stove, and that little tail caught on fire. I looked over in time to see a large flame going up the back of his jacket. My thought was to put out the fire now! My action was I grabbed the flame with my bare hands and put it out. I gently took him out of his vest and sent him to go play in the other room for a while. It was only then that I thought of myself and turned to the sink to run cold water on my hands and check to see the damage. SHOCKED, I saw nothing on my hands. I was thinking there should be blisters at least, if not melted nylon embedded in my skin. I halfway expected to see blood and bone. There was nothing there on my hands, not even redness. As I stared in amazement, I heard God say, "This is the love I am looking for. The love that will respond with no thought to self, and do what is needed to save my children from the fire." Needless to say, I went!

I ended up ministering to prisoners' families. It was challenging, heartbreaking, and rewarding. There were so many of these families depending on the convict to support them. They all lived in severe poverty. I stood and prayed with people in rooms with walls covered by roaches, like wallpaper. I learned for the first time that there are places in America where people live like a third-world country. One man was caring for his mom and his grandparents in a two-room shack filled with squalor. I almost threw up walking in the door when I went to check on their needs. The grandparents were covered in sores, because while he was in prison, his mom did not have the strength to turn them over in bed. I left a box of food and some sheets. I sent the county home health nurse to intervene on their behalf.

I found grandparents living in an abandoned little garage, caring for their son's children with no electricity or heat.

It gets very cold at night in the winter, even in Arizona. The Thanksgiving I was there, it even snowed.

Their son eventually died of a drug overdose and the mother was still in prison. You don't have to leave the country to find heartbreaking needs. The whole experience was shocking and educational. I will never be the same, I am glad to say. I got the electric company to give them electricity for a few months until we found better answers for their plight.

The why you do something is as important to you and God as what you do.

This morning in the shower, God said, "My narrow path and needle gate are things done in relationship with Me, in My love. Did you sense My heart and desire to move in a direction? Did you do something to prove you loved Me, or did My love prove itself through you? The narrow path is My love, My will being accomplished in and through your life. Let My will be done on earth as it is in heaven. The rich young ruler in Matthew 19:16–22 was infatuated and fascinated by what he saw and experienced following Me, but he was not captivated by love with Me."

I understood that if he were captivated by this love, he would have said yes to Jesus and waited for guidance. When you love, would you not give all to the one you love? This ruler walked away, grieving he had so much to give up. I took that to mean no matter how much you have or how good you think you are, if you attach it to yourself, you will not fit through this eye of the needle. Your stuff and your labels are not meaningful there. I did some serious motivational searching.

I tried to imagine what God would have directed him to do. Perhaps he would have started a fishing business and given many people a way to make a living. Perhaps he would have invested in many other people's dreams. There are so many ways to give it all away. Maybe Jesus just wanted him to sense that all he had wasn't just his. Then if he were to give it away, he would have no sense of loss. After all, God did give it to him as a huge blessing for some reason. How sad He missed the adventure of a lifetime because he thought it was money that made him rich and that a title defined him.

There are two scriptures I should quote here. Mathew 7:13–14, "Enter by the narrow gate; for wide *is* the gate and broad *is* the way that leads to destruction, and there are many who go in by it. Because narrow *is* the gate and difficult *is* the way which leads to life, and there are few who find it."

Matthew 19:24: "And again I say to you, it is easier for a camel to go through the eye of a needle than for a rich man to enter the kingdom of God." Don't make the mistake of thinking Jesus does not want you to have things, that is not what He is saying. The rich young ruler in Matthew 19:16–22 had his identity and self-importance defined by his riches and status. He could not separate himself from them.

I often have to examine my motives. Am I responding out of my heart to love, or allegiance to an ideal, or going along with what is a popular belief?

Love certainly does bring an allegiance with its response. If your allegiance comes from your need to belong or fix your identity crisis, or even just duty, it is not always love. All those things come from your head trying to fix

166

you and give you a fulfillment from something other than God's love. It is not from your heart or spiritual growth. It seems the only gift worthy to give God is the one He gave you to give Him. YOU!

Please don't feel condemned by this. We all walk this path on the way to finding our true heart. There is no condemnation in Jesus (Romans 8:1).

The best Bible story to back me up is the prodigal son. You will note in the story the son was not even repentant to go home. He was hungry and naked and wanted the benefits the servants got. There was no, "I love you, Dad. I miss you." It was all the love the Father had for him that got him restored. Son number two was working with the attitude of I earned it more. Jesus's story about the late workers in the fields getting paid the same as the ones who started earlier shows us more the Father's heart.

After serving in my church youth group for a few years, God spoke to me during a service where another minister was asking for helpers. He was going to a juvenile detention center a couple of Sunday afternoons each month. God said, "This is what I have for you right now." I went faithfully. I had it in my mind I had a lot to give because of my past. I could speak firsthand to them. For months, it seemed to go nowhere. Perhaps it was because **I** thought **I** had something!

I went on one last trip with the youth to give an evangelic youth presentation to a town in Idaho. This time, I was asked to go as the cook. I had never cooked for forty-five people. I needed all the God help I could get from my fix-it app to plan food, as well as some advice from friends. We slept on hard gym floors of a church and then a local Salvation Army soup kitchen. This was a real test of my character and Christian spirit. I remember whining to God, "I want to minister and all I am is a cook with an aching back. Why do these people think my food is too rich?" Apparently, I am heavy on the garlic and onions.

The whole experience did change something inside me in spite of my whining. I knew I was serving in the unseen capacity so God could do something awesome in some young peoples' lives on both sides of the outreach. It was not about me.

When we got back, I went back to juvenile detention and said the same things I said before the mission trip, but this time the Holy Spirit showed up big time. Twelve girls were on the floor crying and asking Jesus into their hearts. It started being like that week after week that I went. When my pastor and I sat down to count up the reports I had turned in that year, over 300 young troubled youth had accepted Jesus.

It is still heartbreaking that I could not get in there to disciple them so they could stay walking a better path. There was a very legalistic religious group that had filled that slot a long time ago. I met with one once. They came on the wrong day. This person sat in on my session, and said I should not talk to them about the God I know; after all, they are like animals, they don't appreciate much. That group said I should speak out the rules because that's what they really need. I did not follow their advice. I hope this book finds them.

Someday, perhaps they will figure out rules without relationship breeds rebellion. It is an empty, hurtful thing without a love relationship; it appears to serve very little of a good purpose. It is not the good news we Christians were to bring to the hurting and broken.

Right now, I belong to a group we call The Gathering, because we all come from different churches. Most of us belonged to the same church at one time and attended the same Bible study groups off and on. I helped my group of ladies put together shoe boxes full of things to send to Samaritan's purse. They give them out at Christmas to kids all over the world. These ladies have become my best friends and support group. I have been learning to be a friend, praying and serving them in their times of need, too. We give each other encouraging words, help during a difficulty sickness or surgery, babysitting kids, meals during crises, and serving at memorial services for loved ones gone home. We have shared sorrow, laughter, joy, and birthdays. My favorite is when someone makes something and they show it off. We all ooh and aah! at their accomplishment, and we ring a bell. The atta girl! does wonders for each of us.I am so honored to be apart of these ladies. This is the same group Paul Young calls the possey, who pray for his ministry.

What comfort zones would you be separated from to serve?

Make a list of small servant tasks you could do just this week.

What new person could you smile at this week?

Hug an extra person this week.

Buy something from the kid who knocks on your door.

Pack some lunches and hand them out to street people.

Let us show the world around us the love God puts in us. The one the Holy Spirit shed abroad in our hearts.

MY TWO CENTS' WORTH
(ON WRITING THIS BOOK)

Doing what God asked me to do has been a very enlightening adventure. It has helped me hone in and focus on all that God has really done for me. This experience has expanded my gratitude and ability to be more thankful for the good in the midst of the turmoil of living in a fallen world.

In the beginning, I mentioned I am not a Bible scholar nor do I claim to have the one true answer for everyone's life. I only wanted to inspire those who find it difficult believing in a good God. For those new in faith who find it so overwhelming. I am just another human in the struggle of life. I have inherited much baggage, like many of you. I have made major mistakes, like some of you. I have tried to navigate myself through the maze of choices in life and have come to many dead ends. I know people fault you for not grasping realities that would make better choices and give you a better life. I want you to know you're not the only one who could not see, hear, or comprehend what those were or even still are, in some cases. The Word says we walk in darkness, and even those who have the light see as through a dark glass (1 Corinthians 13:12). The light does get brighter, and seeing gets clearer.

A relationship with the Father of creation, the author and finisher of your life, can and does help. I have found every word He speaks is true, and He is a God who is a man of His word. He asked us to come and learn of Him, His ways, His Spirit, and He would meet us there where we are and take us by the hand and lead us one step at a time. I know that is true because I am living it. I know it is true because God was willing to be born in a human so that the heavenly would be united with man once again, like He intended in the Garden of Eden. Jesus took the time to relate to His human experience in every way. He knows what it is.

When Jesus was raised from the dead and ascended into heaven, he did not go back the same way he came. He went back as a transfigured man, and when we go to heaven, the Bible says we will see him because we shall be like Him. We get a transfigured body, too (1 John 3:2).

Jesus sits on a throne at the right hand of God, and we who faithfully, patiently endure will have surrounding thrones. We get to rule and reign with him. Not sure yet what we rule over, but there are a lot of speculations popping up in my head. I personally only have a desire to rule over my own Garden of Eden.

This journey into eternal life with Jesus takes desire and earnest pursuit. The God of the universe is not casual about the love of His life, which is you. He is purposed in His love and acts. He is a life force ever moving forward with plans that include your dreams and exceed them. He is more than worthy of your devotion and time spent with

Him. You will be delightfully surprised at what you find Him and you doing.

I pray you will open your heart to the Trinity, Father, Son, and Holy Spirit. The world was created out of this loving family community. I hope you choose to agree to be a part of it. I pray the eyes, ears, and heart of your understanding be opened. I hope you will let me know if this book helped you any with your journey.

By the time this book goes to print, I will have a website and blog going, so we can be community and help each other walk out our destinies.

www.heavenstogobox.com

Suggested Help Books

If you are just started on your Journey to know God and the Holy Spirit or just your life heart aches are letting you know that there are tough issues you need to get resolved.

These are some my starting places, to try to understand what God was trying to say and do for me.

Co-dependent No More, Melody Beattie

Healing the inner Child, Charles Whitfield

Adult children of abusive parents, Steven Farmer

Connecting, Larry Crab

Boundaries, Townsend and Cloud

Self Matters, Dr Phil McGraw

The Life Model, Wilder, Khow, Coursey & Sutton

The Way of the Wild Heart, John Eldridge

Captivating, Stacy Eldridge

The Great Dance, Baxter Kruger

The Rhema Code, Scott Shang

Anything that comes out of Bethel temple is a good call

If you're into metaphors;

The Shack, & Crossroads, Paul young

Hind's Feet In High Places, Hannah Harnard

Please read the bible too.

I recommend you pray before you read to ask the Holy Spirit to open you up to what what you need to hear from the Father God who loves you.

ABOUT THE AUTHOR

I was born in Syracuse New York January 1947.   I am married and have 5 grown children.

As of this date I have 8 grand children.

Jesus finally apprehended my heart and soul in March of 1973. I don't think I have ever spent a day since without sensing a need to express His love somehow.

I have worked in the nursery, taught every age of Sunday school at some point. I   was a high school youth group worker. We did several Mexico mission trips with them.

I have spent time in prison ministry and juvenile detention and street ministry.   I co-labored to start a women's recovery center for women with life controlling issues and became the director. As director I was privileged to speak at many places, churches, retreats as well as Women's aglow.

I now enjoy working with a prophetic creative arts group at Destiny Christian Fellowship here in Happy Valley Oregon.

We are newly started and excited about the different ways God is leading us to reach people with His love and truth.

Made in the USA
Monee, IL
27 May 2023

34232704R00098